Praise for *Moving from Fear to Freedom*

"Another winner by Grace Fox! Every woman will identify with *Moving from Fear to Freedom*. With profound insight, humor, sound advice, and amazing stories, Grace inspires you to jump in, face your fears, learn, grow, and come out stronger on the other side. *Moving from Fear to Freedom* will be part of my personal library. It's a keeper."

MARGARET GIBB, PRESIDENT, WOMEN ALIVE

"Grace Fox has tackled a challenging emotion—fear—and written about it with clarity, compassion, and courage. She offers help, hope, and even a bit of humor as she uncovers the truth about fear through real-life stories, relevant Scripture, and steps of practical application. My favorite part of each chapter is Praying the Promises. A must-read for anyone afraid of fear!"

KAREN O'CONNOR, AUTHOR OF *WALKIN' WITH GOD AIN'T FOR WIMPS* AND *THE BEAUTY OF AGING*

"Grace Fox has nailed the fears that pierce a woman's heart and prevent her from experiencing the true joy and freedom that are her birthright as a child of the living God. For too long we women have allowed ourselves to walk in the shadow of fear, missing out on the sunlight that beckons us and is ours for the taking. Grace shows us how we can move from the shadow into the sunlight once and for all and, in turn, help others to do the same.

"Complete with provocative points to ponder, Scriptures to meditate on, and prayers to pray, *Moving from Fear to Freedom* is a must-read book for any woman who desires to live in the truth that "God has not given us a spirit of fear, but of power and of love and of a sound mind."

KATHI MACIAS, AUTHOR OF *HOW CAN I RUN A TIGHT SHIP WHEN I'M SURROUNDED BY LOOSE CANNONS?*

"Grace is far more than an author; she's a friend who lovingly walks beside you through the pages of her book. Her writing takes you to a place of real freedom. Her words are like keys that unlock a woman's spirit and help her to live freely in the truth. Grace presents liberating spiritual principles with clarity and sensitivity. She offers profound truth in a practical way through deep spiritual insights and great storytelling. She is truly a woman of wisdom and compassion, and I am honored to know her."

JENNIFER ROTHSCHILD, SPEAKER ON THE POPULAR
WOMEN OF FAITH TOUR, AUTHOR OF *LESSONS I LEARNED IN THE DARK*

"*Moving from Fear to Freedom* is a deeply soul-satisfying book. Grace Fox does a masterful job of helping us engage our hearts as well as our minds in becoming active participants in taking control of fear and transforming it, with the help of the Holy Spirit, into the energy we need to move more deeply and freely into the abundant life that was Jesus' stated intention of his life. Grace knows what she's talking about and is a trusted 'over coffee' friend. This is a great resource for all ages."

ROBIN CHADDOCK, CERTIFIED LIFE COACH, AUTHOR, SPEAKER

"Grace Fox's book *Moving from Fear to Freedom* is a must-read for every woman regardless of age. Many of the fears resonated with my own life experience, so I could identify with the struggles as well as the freedom of giving all to God. I was reminded of Proverbs 3:5-6—"Trust in the LORD with *all* your heart and lean not on your own understanding; in *all* your ways acknowledge Him, and He will make your paths straight."

DEB HAGGERTY, POPULAR AUTHOR AND SPEAKER

"There really is an upside to fear! Grace Fox shares this truth by revealing her own struggles with fear along with real, from-the-heart stories of women across the country. The sections at the end of each chapter—Points for Progress, Promises to Ponder, and Praying the Promises—are creative and brilliant practical helps. Grace clearly demonstrates that fear does indeed take flight in the face of God's infinite person and power! Personally, I thank Grace for helping me to so deeply understand and face fear in a whole new way. This book has brought me into the freedom God so desires for all of us."

LANE P. JORDAN, AUTHOR OF *12 STEPS TO BECOMING A MORE ORGANIZED WOMAN* AND *12 STEPS TO BECOMING A MORE ORGANIZED MOM*

Moving
from Fear *to*
Freedom

Grace Fox

HARVEST HOUSE PUBLISHERS

EUGENE, OREGON

Grace Fox: Published in association with the Books & Such Literary Agency, 52 Mission Circle, Suite 122, PMB 170, Santa Rosa, CA 95409-5370, www.booksandsuch.biz.

All emphases and insertions in Scripture quotations are added by the author.

This book contains stories in which the author has changed some people's names and some details of their situations in order to protect their privacy.

Cover by Left Coast Design, Portland, Oregon

Cover photo © LWA / Photographer's Choice / Getty Images

MOVING FROM FEAR TO FREEDOM
Copyright © 2007 by Grace Fox
Published by Harvest House Publishers
Eugene, Oregon 97402
www.harvesthousepublishers.com

Library of Congress Cataloging-in-Publication Data
Fox, Grace, 1958-
Moving from fear to freedom / Grace Fox.
p. cm.
ISBN 978-0-7369-1944-9 (pbk.)
1. Fear—Religious aspects—Christianity. 2. Peace of mind—Religious aspects—Christianity. I. Title.
BV4908.5.F69 2007
248.8'6—dc22

2007002498

Printed in the United States of America

10 11 12 13 14 15 / VP-SK / 12 11 10 9 8 7 6 5 4 3

ACKNOWLEDGMENTS

✦ ✦ ✦

I wish to thank the courageous women who opened their hearts and told their stories in this book. Their honesty has enriched my life, and I pray it will do the same for yours. Their journeys offer hope and testify to God's awesome ability to deliver us from our fears.

I also wish to thank my prayer team. The project is complete, thanks to their prayers on my behalf. They truly are a stellar group.

Thanks to my literary agent, Wendy Lawton, and to the Harvest House staff for their partnership. Thanks also to the retailers for introducing this book to their customers—theirs is a frontline ministry.

And a big thanks to my husband, Gene, for listening to me as I pondered ideas aloud and for giving me daily encouragement.

CONTENTS

✦ ✦ ✦

The *Upside* of Fear

Dear Reader,

I admit it—fear is no stranger to me. My earliest recollection of its presence in my life traces back to my preschool days. At that time, my family lived in Alberta, about 40 minutes' drive from an area famous for dinosaur fossils. My imagination worked overtime, especially if I woke during the night. I was sure that a dinosaur lived under my bed and that it would grab my ankles if I dared step onto the floor.

My childish thinking told me that leaving my room meant losing my life. So rather than fall prey to the Tyrannosaurus rex, I'd stand on my bed and take a flying leap toward the door to get beyond its grasp. My strategy obviously worked—I'm still alive and have two ankles to prove it!

Fear stayed with me when I graduated from kindergarten and entered elementary school. My mom occasionally asked me to fetch a jar of peaches or pickles from the basement storage room. I obliged, but only after mustering every ounce of courage within my skinny frame. I was certain that girl-eating monsters lived in the basement and that they could outrun me on the stairs. I ascended those stairs two by two, terrified that if I did anything less, I'd become a monster's meal.

As a grown woman, I can look back on those fears and laugh. But nowadays I face other fears that are anything but funny. I've worried about my kids' well-being. I've fretted over our bank account. I've stewed over feeling inadequate, and I've panicked when personal storms have blown in and threatened to shake my world.

Can you relate?

Be honest—I know you understand what I'm talking about. In preparing to write this book, I conducted a survey wherever I spoke at women's events. The results only confirmed what I suspected—I'm not the only woman who struggles with negative fear. It affects women of all ages and from all walks of life, often signaling its presence by provoking apprehension, premature wrinkles, stomach pains, tension headaches, and sleepless nights. If left to run rampant, it can rob us of joy and the power-filled life that God intends for us.

As I began studying examples of fear in the Bible, I discovered a fascinating truth: The first reference to fear is found in Genesis 3:8-10. It says, "Toward evening they [Adam and Eve] heard the LORD God walking about in the garden, so they hid themselves among the trees. The LORD God called to Adam, 'Where are you?' He replied, 'I heard you, so I hid. I was *afraid* because I was naked.'"

Fear was not a part of God's agenda for His creation, but it slithered onto the scene when Adam and Eve sinned. It became a wedge between them and the One who created them for relationship with Himself.

Unfortunately, fear is still on the scene today. It can interfere with our relationship with God, just as it did for Adam and Eve. Or—here's the exciting part—it can be the catalyst for a deeper relationship with Him. Every time we're afraid, we can either forget faith and try to do things our way (as if that's really going to work!), or we can acknowledge our fear and call out to God for help. When He answers, we experience Him in new ways. That's the upside of fear.

Life is too short to spend it battling fear and its negative effects. Besides, God has better things in store for us. He wants us to embrace each day wholeheartedly and make every minute count. He wants us to live to our full potential and leave a mark on coming generations. He wants us to impact our families, our churches, our communities, and ultimately the world for Himself. I want that too. Do you?

If so, this book is for you. You'll be inspired by the real-life stories of other women who have faced their fears and discovered new truths about God. You'll be challenged as you see how biblical heroes and heroines dealt with fear. And you'll be encouraged as you learn what God's Word says about fear and how to rise above it.

At the end of each chapter you'll find several practical helps. First is a section called Points for Progress. These questions are designed for individual or group study and will help you apply truth and experience deeper personal growth.

Next you'll find a section called Promises to Ponder. Copy these Scriptures on recipe cards and post them where you'll see them often—on the fridge, near your kitchen sink, on the dashboard of your car, on the bathroom mirror, near your computer, or beside your baby's changing table. Filling our minds with the truth of God's Word equips us to face fearful situations when they come along. His Word renews our minds and helps us to view life from His eternal perspective rather than from our own limited point of view. Fear takes flight in the face of God's infinite person and power!

You'll also find a section called Praying the Promises in which I've turned those Bible verses into prayers. Pray them for yourself or on behalf of others struggling with fear. God promises to hear those whose hearts belong to Him and who ask anything in line with His will (1 John 3:21-22; 5:14). We know beyond a doubt that He wants His children to overcome their fears, so we can pray with confidence and expect Him to answer.

As I've written this book, my understanding of the potential negative impact of fear on my life has grown. But so has my understanding of the upside of fear. I pray that from this day forward, God will enable me to view fear in a different light—as a tool in His hands that will help me experience Him in new ways and move into freedom. I pray the same for you!

I invite you to e-mail me about how God has used this book in your life. We can encourage each other in our spiritual journey. In fact, give a copy of this book to a friend or donate one to your church library. Ask your public librarians to bring it in so that other women in your community can benefit from its message. Let's live life the way God intended—in rest and relationship with Him. And let's make a difference in the world around us.

By the way, I write a free monthly online newsletter called *Growing with Grace.* If you'd like to receive it, simply visit my website, click on the free e-zine link, and follow the directions. I hope you enjoy it!

Know you are loved,

Grace

www.gracefox.com

1

The Faces *of* Fear

You gain strength, courage, and confidence by every
experience in which you really stop and look fear in the face.

ELEANOR ROOSEVELT

Fear—every woman struggles or has struggled with it in one form or another, and few dare to admit it. Why? We're afraid to! If we confess to wrestling with fear, others might think less of us. Besides, we've been brought up to believe that it doesn't bother good Christians. We're supposed to have strong faith—strong enough to move mountains.

Rather than admit our real feelings when our faith wavers and fear takes over, we often bury ourselves in busyness or flash a fake smile and pretend everything's okay. Unwilling to identify and acknowledge our fear, we succumb to feelings of failure and powerlessness.

Ladies, it's time to change!

Fear is our worst enemy. We can let it ruin us by filling our minds with thoughts of dread and woe, or we can face it head-on and use it as a tool that can empower us by drawing us into a deeper understanding of who God is. My purpose for writing this book is to help others learn to face it and use it as a tool.

I'm not a psychologist, however, so I'm not pretending to give

11

clinical advice. I'm an ordinary woman who, through life experience, has encountered the face of fear more than a few times. I've felt my heart race and my adrenalin rush at the sound of things going bump in the night. I've wrestled privately with the fear of rejection—*What will others think of me if they know what I'm really like?* I've panicked when my journey has taken detours into unknown territory, and I've trembled when sensing God asking me to walk a path too risky for my liking.

In the past, fear has rendered me sleepless at night and snappy toward my husband and kids. It's caused me to say no to too many opportunities. I believe it was even responsible for a mysterious rash on my arms when I was in junior high.

Back then, our family considered moving to a new city. The thought of leaving friends and familiarity terrified me. An itchy red rash broke out on my arms. When it wouldn't go away, I saw a medical doctor. He asked a few questions and prescribed tranquilizers. The drugs did the trick, but we never addressed the root of my problem—fear.

In the past, fear has played havoc in my thoughts and caused me to second-guess God. But no more. I'm done with it. I know that God has a better way for me to live than in fear's clutches, and I choose to pursue His plan and purpose.

Speaking at women's events has given me the opportunity to address the fear issue and see its far-reaching impact. Before writing this book, I asked nearly 350 women to name the fears they struggle with. Some signed their names on their papers, but many did not—perhaps the fear of being identified restrained them. Here's a smattering of their responses:

> Abandonment.

> My husband was not a Christian when I married him. He was on active duty in the U.S. Navy, and as the day approached for him to be deployed, I feared that, in

the worst-case scenario, he would die without knowing Jesus.

I had an affair. My husband knows, and we're working things out. But no one else knows, none of our friends or family. No one. I feel like I can't talk to even my best friend about what's happened within me. Every day is a battle.

We lived in a twelfth-story apartment for a few months. The balcony truly scared me. I was afraid my baby might fall from it.

I'm dealing with cancer, and I struggle with the fear that my son, age 15, and daughter, age 12, will be harmed by watching me go through this. I don't want to miss their growing up. I struggle to remember that God is in control.

My life has been wonderful with only small challenges. I fear that the Lord may cause some catastrophic event to help me grow. I'm a wimp—I want to grow in easy ways.

Because of the way my daughters-in-law were raised, I fear losing relationships with my grown sons.

My kids take up so much of my time that I fear losing connection with my husband. I fear not knowing him when my kids leave home.

My mom died before I had kids. I fear raising children without her advice or help.

I'm getting older and still haven't married. I fear remaining single for the rest of my life.

I fear marriage because my folks had a lousy relationship.

I fear what might happen if my husband doesn't get a job before our money runs out.

I fear that my children will make poor choices and pay harsh consequences.

I fear not being able to conceive.

My husband has multiple sclerosis, and I'm afraid of what the future holds.

The list goes on and on, penned by women ages 19 to 80 representing various cultures. Some of these gals are stay-at-home moms. Others are single parents, business women, pastors' wives, missionaries, or grandmothers. Some have whopping bank accounts. Others survive on social assistance.

Each answer is as unique as the woman who wrote it, but most fall into specific categories such as fear about our children's well-being, fear of an unknown future, and fear of financial insecurity. As you read this book, you'll find that the chapters expose the most common faces of fear. My prayer is that whatever fears you face, you'll find the stories and teachings relevant to your situation.

Are you ready to move from fear to freedom with me? If so, let's go!

Fear Defined

Let's begin with a basic understanding of fear. Webster's dictionary offers three definitions of fear as a verb: (1) "to be afraid of," (2) "to be in awe of," and (3) "to expect with misgiving."

It's easy to relate to the first definition because we've all felt afraid of something or someone at sometime. Kim, my 20-year-old daughter, is afraid of having her blood drawn for medical tests. Her face turns white, and she nearly faints when the needle is inserted. (We've learned, by experience, that she ought to lie down rather than sit in a chair when this procedure is done!) We haven't got a clue as to why she's so afraid of needles. She just is.

I'm afraid of big barking dogs because several mangy mutts tried to make me their meal when I delivered newspapers in eighth grade. Nearly four decades have passed, but I still remember the adrenaline rush I experienced when a German shepherd lunged at me and plastered his muddy paw prints on the back of my winter jacket. Even today, walking past my neighbors' homes when their dogs are loose requires all my courage. The first sight of a woofing, free-wheeling canine kicks me into prayer mode: *Lord, please, please, p-l-e-a-s-e keep me safe.*

I have other fears too, such as driving on icy roads and sailing in extremely high winds. I consider them dangers that pose a potential threat to my physical safety, so I choose to avoid them.

Now you know my fears. How about you? What are you afraid of? Think of your own situation. Fill in the blank. "I am afraid of
_____."

The second definition—"to be in awe of"—describes how we should regard God. We ought to fear Him because of His holiness and power and wisdom. This doesn't mean we're afraid of Him, although we have reason to be if we're deliberately choosing to disobey His commands. Being in awe of Him means that we revere Him. We hold Him in high esteem because of who He is.

The third definition—"to expect with misgiving"—describes a sense of uneasiness or disquiet. We can relate to that one as well if we've ever focused on a particular situation and worried about its potential outcome.

Many parents experience this when their eldest child begins driving alone. They know the child has passed the driving exam, the vehicle is in good working condition, and the roads are clear. But still...a nagging uneasiness haunts the parents until both child and car return intact.

A list of synonyms for *fear* lends several vivid descriptions. To fear is to falter, lose courage, be alarmed, have qualms about, cower, shrink, tremble, and—my favorite—break out in a sweat.

Can you relate to any of these synonyms? Perhaps you've lost your courage while facing a terminal illness. Maybe you've faltered in praying for a wayward child because you've prayed for years without seeing results. Perhaps you've cowered in a corner, afraid that your friends might abandon you if they discover a hidden secret, such as a homosexual lifestyle. Maybe you've been tempted to shrink back when someone asked you to do a task for which you didn't feel qualified, or you've had qualms about your child's relationship with a particular member of the opposite sex.

If you can relate to these synonyms, take heart. You're not alone! Your specific circumstances may be different from the ones I mentioned, but the feelings they trigger are the same, and they're all based in fear.

Types of Fear

Women of all ages and from all walks of life encounter two basic types of fear—destructive and constructive. The latter is beneficial. Here are a few snapshots of how this appears in real life:

- The fear of being run over causes us to look both ways before crossing the street. We instill that fear into our kids at a young age!

- The fear of an empty gas tank prompts us to stop at a gas station and fill 'er up.

- The fear of a house fire prompts us to make sure we turn off the stove burners and the coffeemaker before we leave home.

- The fear of lung cancer keeps us from smoking or prompts us to stop.

- The fear of breast cancer encourages us to do monthly self-examinations and have annual mammograms when we reach the appropriate age. (Well, at least it should!)

- The fear of obesity, diabetes, and heart disease causes us to eliminate junk food and eat nutritious meals. (Ditto—at least it should!)

Constructive fear can prove helpful. It steers us toward wise decisions and actions. It promotes self-preservation and can literally save our lives. We'll place reverential fear in this category. It inspires a healthy fear of God and encourages us to make wise choices and live in a manner that pleases Him.

Destructive fear, on the other hand, is another story. If left unchecked, it can cause sleeplessness, illness, and chronic worry. It can hinder our ability to make decisions and perform even mundane tasks. It can paralyze us, rob us of joy and peace, and cause stress and ulcers.

Phobias fall into this category. One dictionary defines a phobia as an "intense, abnormal, or illogical fear of a specified thing."[1] We've heard of claustrophobia—the fear of confined spaces—and arachnophobia—the fear of spiders. But I found a list of numerous less-known phobias.

For instance, mageirocophobia is the fear of cooking. (I'm writing this after 5:00 p.m., and I still don't know what to fix for dinner. Perhaps I should plead mageirocophobia tonight!) Then there's hypegiaphobia—the fear of responsibility. Try this one: ephebiphobia—the fear of teenagers. And then there's anglophobia—the fear of England or English culture. And bibliophobia—the fear of books (obviously not an issue you struggle with!). And finally, phobophobia—you guessed it, the fear of phobias.

According to the National Institute of Mental Health (NIMH), nearly 11.5 million American adults suffer from phobias. More than 19 million American adults are affected by anxiety disorders annually. The NIMH describes these disorders as follows:

- *Panic disorders.* "Repeated episodes of intense fear that strike often and without warning." Symptoms include chest pain, shortness of breath, dizziness, fear of dying, and abdominal distress.

- *Obsessive-compulsive disorder.* "Repeated, unwanted thoughts or compulsive behaviors that seem impossible to stop or control."

- *Post-traumatic stress disorder.* "Persistent symptoms that occur after experiencing or witnessing a traumatic event such as rape or other criminal assault, war, child abuse, natural or human-caused disasters, or crashes." Symptoms include anger, irritability, nightmares, numbed emotions, and flashbacks.

- *Phobias.* Two major types of phobias are social phobias and specific phobias. Social phobias result in a disabling fear of embarrassment or humiliation in social settings and lead to the avoidance of many pleasurable experiences. Isolation becomes a risk and can lead to depression or alcoholism. Specific phobias are characterized by an irrational fear of a situation or object that poses little or no real danger, such as spiders. Sufferers limit their lives to avoid the object of their fears.

- *Generalized anxiety disorder.* "Constant, exaggerated worrisome thoughts and tension about everyday routine life events and activities, lasting at least six months. Almost always anticipating the worst even though there is little reason to expect it." Symptoms include muscle tension, fatigue, nausea, and headache.[2]

Destructive fears can control our minds, attitudes, and behaviors. But we can overcome them! A professional counselor's insights and recommendations might help. And of course, we should always delve into God's Word to see what it says about any issue.

Fear's Effect

I've given you a brief overview of the scientific face of fear and some of the different effects it can have on people's lives. Now let's zoom in for a closer look.

"The only thing we have to fear is fear itself—nameless, unreasoning, unjustified, terror which paralyzes needed efforts to convert retreat to advance," said Franklin D. Roosevelt in his first inaugural address.

Roosevelt's statement accurately describes fear's effect. If we let it, fear paralyzes us and prevents us from making progress in our lives. It stunts our growth. It locks us into position and declares, *You're not goin' anywhere, sister.*

Been there. Actually, I'm still there. I was a high school senior when my older sister and her best friend took me snow skiing in beautiful Banff, Alberta. They'd both skied before and loved it, but this was my first experience. After two practice runs down the bunny hill, they felt confident about their ability to move on. "C'mon, Grace, you can do it too," they said.

I assessed the situation. Two trips down the bunny hill hardly qualified me to move to a steeper slope, especially when I hadn't even mastered the art of catching the lift without falling on my face. But, impulsive soul that I am, I agreed.

The view from the top nearly took my breath away, but it wasn't because of the scenery. My sister and her friend completed two runs in the time it took me to muster the courage to shove off.

Everything went well for the first few seconds. I glided a few feet and then cut to the left. I skied another few feet and cut to the right, trying hard to look like a pro. It didn't work. When the time came to cut to the left again, my ankles refused to cooperate. Rather than turning, I headed straight down the slope.

Speed and panic gained momentum. My ski poles flapped like broken wings. The ski lift on my left and the trees on my right blurred. Straight ahead, at the bottom of the slope, I saw a snowplow, a small wooden building, and the line of skiers waiting to get on the lift, and I wondered which one I would slam into first.

Scenes from my life zipped through my mind. Dying hadn't been on my agenda when I left my parents' home that morning. Neither was ending my day as a quadriplegic. But now I feared the worst. What could I do?

Pray!

Eloquence loses its importance when one's life is whizzing before one's eyes. Forgetting all inhibitions, I hollered for heavenly help: *God! You made this mountain! I'm gonna die unless You do something quick! H-e-e-e-l-p!*

I didn't even have time to close with a proper amen. About six feet from the lift line, my ski tips crossed each other, and I landed in a heap, sprawled facedown before a gawking crowd. I stopped so abruptly that I have no recollection about how it felt. I do remember lying there and wondering, *Am I still alive?* Then I heard a stranger's voice say, "Are you all right?"

I wiggled one arm and then the other. I stretched one leg and then the other. Everything felt okay physically. But my pride…oh, the pain. At least I could have broken a leg after putting on a show like that for my audience. But noooo, my body was intact. I desperately wanted to stay there, my face imbedded in a snow bank, but the lack of bodily injury gave me no excuse.

"Wow—that was some ride," said another stranger as I struggled to my feet, avoiding the onlookers' stares.

"Yeah, a real rush," I said. "Want me to show you how it's done?"

I've dared to snow ski twice since that incident nearly 30 years ago. It just doesn't work for me. I'm a liability, a hazard to the bunny hill innocents. My high school experience scarred me for life, I'm afraid. Yep, that's the problem—I'm afraid. And fear of being killed or of maiming someone else on the ski slope has held me back from enjoying the sport with my family. I tell them that someone has to guard our family's lunch cooler in the lodge, and I'm happy to volunteer.

Some readers will empathize completely. You too are happy sipping hot chocolate while babysitting the lunch cooler. Others won't relate at all. Careening down a mountain slope at breakneck speeds brings sheer delight. You go, girl! But be honest. Do you have a hidden fear that paralyzes you in a different way?

Perhaps someone has invited you to sing in public. You'd love to oblige, but the mere thought of performing sends shivers up your spine, so you refuse the invitation.

Maybe a woman in your church has been trying to establish a meaningful friendship with you, but you've experienced the pain of rejection once and don't want to feel it again. Rather than make yourself vulnerable, you hide behind your busyness or communicate with her in shallow terms only.

Maybe your husband is abusing you. If you leave him, you won't have a home or source of income. You desperately want help, but fear of reprisal or of being unfairly criticized by others prevents you from telling anyone about your pain.

Perhaps a certain behavior or addiction—overeating, pornography, or perfectionism—holds you captive. You realize your need to escape its grip, but that requires change, and change can be scary. Rather than moving from fear to freedom, you remain mired in the muck. Fear has locked you into position and declared, *You're not goin' anywhere, sister.*

Break Free!

Some folks think they can escape fear's grip on their lives by gaining control of their circumstances. They work harder, play harder, and pray harder, trying to manipulate people and events so they can feel comfortable and predict outcomes. Unfortunately, that doesn't work.

Bruce Larson points out the uselessness of this approach: "We think we can get our lives organized to the place where fear is eliminated. The fallacy here is that we believe we are in control and that by our efforts we can manipulate almost everything around us: family, friends, even circumstances. Obviously, we can't."[3]

Some people try to escape by blaming others for their fear-filled outlook. Rather than assuming responsibility for their attitudes, they blame their parents for raising them incorrectly, they blame their bosses for being too demanding, and they blame the authorities for not doing a good job of protecting them.

I heard about a woman who cared for her 92-year-old mother. As her mother's health deteriorated and she required more assistance, the daughter became frustrated. "Why didn't you look after yourself when you were younger? If you had, you wouldn't have all these problems now," she said.

The daughter's accusation wasn't true. Her frustration was actually based not in irritation with her mother, but in her own fear of the unknown. Anxious thoughts haunted her day and night. *How much medical attention will my mother require as her health declines? How will that affect my other responsibilities? Will my mom's finances cover her expenses? What will life be like without her? Will I be in her situation someday?* Rather than face her fear and assume responsibility for her attitudes and actions, the daughter blamed her mother.

Some folks try to escape their fear by drinking alcohol or taking drugs. They party hearty, enjoying temporary relief but waking up with a big fat headache in the morning, or they find themselves stuck in addictions that land them on a dead-end road. These supposed solutions don't work, so what does?

I believe that the key to unlocking fear's chains is a proper understanding of the character of God. I'm not talking about an understanding based merely on our feelings or what we think is true—we might think we're right but in reality be terribly deceived by society's subtle teachings. I'm talking about understanding God's character as He's revealed it in the truth of His Word. His own declarations and the accounts recorded by the writers of long ago comprise the only trustworthy revelation of who God is.

First John 4:16-18 shows more clearly than any other passage the relationship between fear and the character of God:

> We know how much God loves us, and we have put our trust in him. God is love, and all who live in love live in God, and God lives in them. And as we live in God, our love grows more perfect. So we will not be afraid on the day of judgment, but we can face him with confidence

because we are like Christ here in this world. Such love has no fear because perfect love expels all fear. If we are afraid, it is for fear of judgment, and this shows that his love has not been perfected in us.

Some commentators say these verses teach that those who have a personal relationship with God no longer need to dread standing before Him on the judgment day. He loves us and has forgiven our sins; therefore, we have confidence before Him. If we fear standing before Him on the judgment day, we haven't come to know and understand His love and forgiveness.

But do these verses apply to us and the fears we face while living here on earth as well? Indeed they do. Think about it for a moment...

God is love. Nothing can alter that fact. Love is who He is, and everything He does or allows throughout all of eternity flows from this aspect of His character. If you're like me, you find the full implications of this truth challenging to grasp.

Our finite minds tend to compare God's love to the earthly love we've known. That's like comparing elephants to daisies, especially if we've been rejected by a lover or abused or ignored by our earthly father. They share nothing in common. Human love can be warm and wonderful, but it can sometimes be conditional or controlling. It often disappoints. It often brings pain. But God's love is perfect in every way.

Accepting the truth of God's perfect love by faith, regardless of our feelings, enables us to find rest in His care and sovereignty. Whatever happens, He won't abandon us. He won't hang us out to dry. He won't turn His back on us when we need Him most. That knowledge gives us the courage to face our fears. "Perfect love expels all fear."

God's Word is filled with promises about His constant love. Romans 8:38-39 is just one example:

> And I am convinced that nothing can ever separate us from his love. Death can't, and life can't. The angels

can't, and the demons can't. Our fears for today, our
worries about tomorrow, and even the powers of hell
can't keep God's love away. Whether we are high above
the sky or in the deepest ocean, nothing in all creation
will ever be able to separate us from the love of God that
is revealed in Christ Jesus our Lord.

The apostle Paul wrote these verses, and he did so with authority
born of experience. During his ministry, he endured court trials,
whippings, imprisonment, snakebites, shipwreck, and more. But
regardless of what happened, he remained convinced of God's steadfast love for him. In the midst of our frightening circumstances, can
we say, as Paul did, that we're convinced of God's love for us?

The Scriptures teach us that God's love for us measures far
beyond our wildest imagination. I remember, as a little girl in
Sunday school, singing an action chorus that described this love—as
wide as the ocean, as high as the heavens, as deep as the deepest sea.
Growing up on the prairies left me with little firsthand knowledge
of the sea, so I sang those words with an academic understanding
only. Unfortunately, that's also how I understood God's love for
most of my adult life—merely academically. Thankfully, God is
changing that.

Today my family lives on Canada's west coast, and the sea brings
me a constant visual reminder of the great expanse of God's love.
One of my favorite places to visit is Tofino, a town on the west side
of Vancouver Island. Its surfing, fishing, and sandy beaches beckon
tourists from around the world.

Our family once spent Thanksgiving in Tofino. Gene and I sat
for hours on a rocky point, talking and gazing across the horizon.
We saw nothing but water—endless in its expanse.

Could we measure the sea as it stretched to the far horizon and
beyond? No. Could we gaze heavenward and measure the distance
between the sky and where we sat? No. Could we measure the

water's depths and touch the ocean floor? No. Such is the Father's love for you and me. Beyond measure. Fathomless.

God is love. Can we trust Him with our lives? Can we trust Him even when we don't understand our circumstances? Can we trust Him when others abandon us? Yes, yes, a thousand times yes. Because God is love and He loves us, we can trust Him at all times. Perfect love casts out fear.

Janice's Story

Janice's life proves that understanding God's love can break fear's chains. She grew up in a home where her parents professed to be born-again believers, but life behind closed doors was anything but pretty. Spankings with a leather strap left red welts on her arms and buttocks. Her mother, a bitter woman, often exploded in angry fits and yelled, "I wish you'd never been born!" Her folks provided for her physical needs, but they rarely hugged or kissed her. She felt like an inconvenience. She convinced herself that she could never please her parents, regardless of how hard she tried.

JESUS LOVES ME
ANNA B. WARNER

Jesus loves me! this I know,
For the Bible tells me so;
Little ones to Him belong;
They are weak, but He is strong.

Jesus loves me! He who died,
Heaven's gate to open wide;
He will wash away my sin,
Let His little child come in.

Jesus loves me! loves me still,
Though I'm very weak and ill;
From His shining throne on high,
Comes to watch me where I lie.

Jesus loves me! He will stay
Close beside me all the way;
If I love Him, when I die
He will take me home on high.

Yes, Jesus loves me,
Yes, Jesus loves me,
Yes, Jesus loves me,
The Bible tells me so.

After high school graduation, Janice left home believing she was unlovable. She sought to dispel those feelings through relationships with guys. Each relationship was marred by inappropriate physical involvement and eventually broke up. Her heart was left tattered; her hopes for finding true love, shattered.

For years, Janice wandered through an emotional and spiritual wasteland. She read the Bible, attended church, participated in church programs, and heard sermons and songs that reassured her of God's love, but her heart didn't absorb the truth. One day, her weary soul could survive no longer. She cried a simple prayer to God: *Help me! Show me Your love!* And He did.

Several weeks later, Janice visited an older woman from her church. The woman, sensing Janice's struggle, encouraged her to believe that God had created her for a purpose and that He wanted an intimate friendship with her. During their conversation, the woman quoted Jeremiah 31:3: "I have loved you, my people, with an everlasting love. With unfailing love I have drawn you to myself."

Janice had heard that verse before, but this time it came alive. *God loves me,* she thought. *He really loves me!* She continued reading her Bible as she'd done for years, but as she did, verses about God's unfailing love seemed to leap off its pages. Worship songs took on new meaning. Her prayer life turned from rote recitation to meaningful conversation with God. She began recognizing signs of His love for her in the beauty of creation—singing birds, flowers of every imaginable color and shape, and furry friends. She began acknowledging His love expressed through the kindness of her church family and through the words the older woman spoke.

As Janice grew in her understanding of God's character, her fear of being unlovable subsided. Her confidence increased. She found the courage to tell her story and discovered others who struggled with the same issue.

"Understanding God's unconditional and everlasting love has transformed my life," says Janice. "I no longer fear being rejected or being unlovable. God's love has filled me with joy."

Perhaps you can relate to Janice's situation. Your particulars may be different, but you may have suffered similar pain. The bad news is that fear wants to hold you hostage. The good news is that God's love can set you free.

✦ POINTS FOR PROGRESS ✦

1. Describe a situation that caused you to fear.

2. Which synonym for fear most accurately describes how you felt in the midst of that situation? Did you cower? Lose courage? Falter? Did you break into a sweat?

3. Psalm 118:4-8 (NIV) contains truths that reinforce what we've learned in this chapter. Read these verses and then answer the questions:

> Let those who fear the LORD say:
> "His love endures forever."
> In my anguish I cried to the LORD,
> and he answered by setting me free.
> The LORD is with me; I will not be afraid.
> What can man do to me?
> The LORD is with me; he is my helper.
> I will look in triumph on my enemies.
> It is better to take refuge in the LORD
> than to trust in man.

- To what truth about God's character are we to testify?

- To whom are we to cry out when we feel afraid? How will He respond?

- What effect should God's presence have on our heart condition?

- What is causing you to be fearful? Fear of an unknown future? Fear of abandonment? Fear for your kids' well-being?

- What promise do these verses contain regarding those fears?

4. Reread "Jesus Loves Me." According to the lyrics, how has Christ shown His love for us?

5. What difference does (should) that make in your life today?

✦ PROMISES TO PONDER ✦

And I pray that Christ will be more and more at home in your hearts as you trust in him. May your roots go down deep into the soil of God's marvelous love. And may you have the power to understand, as all God's people should, how wide, how long, how high, and how deep his love really is. May you experience the love of Christ, though it is so great you will never fully understand it. Then you will be filled with the fullness of life and power that comes from God (Ephesians 3:17-19).

Don't count on your warhorse to give you victory—
    for all its strength, it cannot save you.
But the LORD watches over those who fear him,
    those who rely on his unfailing love.
He rescues them from death
    and keeps them alive in times of famine.
We depend on the LORD alone to save us.
    Only he can help us, protecting us like a shield.
In him our hearts rejoice,
    for we are trusting in his holy name (Psalm 33:17-22).

Don't be troubled. You trust God, now trust in me (John 14:1).

✦ PRAYING THE PROMISES ✦

Heavenly Father, I want You to be more and more at home in my heart, so please teach me to trust You more. Sink my roots down deep into the soil of Your marvelous love. Grant me the power to understand the full scope and dimensions of Your love. And please grant me the privilege of experiencing Christ's love firsthand. For then I will know what it means to be filled with the fullness of life and power that comes from You. Amen.

Dear God, I praise You for Your unfailing love and depend on You alone to save me. Thank You for promising to watch over me because I fear You. Thank You for promising to rescue me from death and for protecting me like a shield. My heart rejoices in You, and I trust Your holy name. I put my hope in You alone; please surround me with Your unfailing love. Amen.

Father God, I praise You for being trustworthy. Keep my heart steadfast. Do not let it be troubled, for I choose to trust in You. Amen.

2
Our Kids' Well-Being

---

*Ultimately we know deeply that on the
other side of every fear is a freedom.*

MARILYN FERGUSON

My husband's words stunned me. "This can't be happening," I whispered. Hot tears rolled down my cheeks. Gene took my hands in his. His eyes met mine. "We'll get through this," he said. I longed to believe him, but in all honesty, fear overwhelmed me.

It was March 20, 1985. The day before, I'd given birth to our second child, Stephanie—a sister for our 20-month-old son, Matthew. But minutes after my Cesarean delivery, a doctor examined our baby's swollen head. "Hydrocephalus," he said. "Excess water on the brain. For her sake, you must return to the United States as soon as possible."

The diagnosis knocked our world off its axis. Our newborn required neurosurgery to drain the excess fluid and reduce the risk of brain damage. A shunt inserted into her head would alleviate the pressure. Trouble was, we were living in Nepal—a country where children with hydrocephalus die without advanced medical technology.

For nearly three years prior, Gene had used his civil engineering skills to promote rural economic development in that land. I'd taught basic health care among our Brahmin villagers. The first two years were wrought with homesickness and culture shock, but we'd grown to love the Nepalese and had committed our lives to working among them. In fact, the week before Stephanie's birth, we'd had a personnel interview with a career mission agency. Now this.

In an instant, our focus changed from making future plans to doing whatever was necessary to save our baby's life. But the doctor's diagnosis wasn't the only trauma facing us.

Coworkers had contacted a travel agent on our behalf and requested tickets on the first flight from Kathmandu to the United States. The agent said there were only two seats left—not enough for our family and Gene's mom, who had arrived a few days earlier to lend grandmotherly help. "Besides," added the agent, "the infant passenger is less than a week old; flying at that age is against airline policy. And the mother has just had major surgery. She's considered high risk, so she's not allowed on the plane either."

Gene knelt beside my chair and relayed this information as gently as possible. Initial shock evolved into anger. Questions swirled through my mind: *Forget the stupid rules! How can an airline do this? My baby will die if she doesn't have neurosurgery!* Anger dissolved into feelings of utter helplessness.

Gene wrapped his arms around me. "We'll get through this," he reassured me again. "I have a plan. You'll stay here with my mom and Matthew until the next available flight. I'll take Stephanie to the States."

"You can't do that," I said through broken sobs. "I'm nursing her. I must go with her."

"You're in no condition to travel halfway around the world," he answered.

I wanted to argue, but I knew he was right. Surgery had left me in crippling pain. Traveling 12,000 miles, especially while caring for a critically ill newborn, was out of the question.

Gene helped me into bed and returned to packing our meager household belongings. I watched Stephanie as she slept nearby in a wicker bassinet. Fear-filled thoughts swirled through my mind: *Will this child survive? If she does, what will her quality of life be? And if she doesn't...?*

A Common Factor

Mothers worldwide share a common denominator—we want the best for our children. We want them to prosper as they develop physically, mentally, emotionally, and spiritually. We want them to grow into responsible adults, wise yet innocent in the world's ways. We want them to be safe and free from the consequences of other people's evil choices and from negative circumstances beyond their control.

In addition to desiring our children's best, however, many of us share another commonality—fear for their well-being. We feel what Aristotle called the "pain that arises from the anticipation of evil." From colic to kindergarten to college and beyond, we worry about what-ifs, and our minds conjure up an amazing array of negative scenarios. *What if my son has difficulty adjusting to his new school? What if my teenager can't find a summer job? What if my daughter gets hurt at summer camp?*

My kids have all left the nest, or in our case, the Foxes' den. Now they're cooking for themselves. I encourage them toward a healthy diet, but in reality, I haven't got a clue if they're eating anything other than macaroni and cheese. Perhaps their menus mimic the one my husband enjoyed while he was in college: frozen corn for dinner one night a week, boiled potatoes another night, a fried pork chop the next. To this day, he grins and says that by the end of each week, he'd had a well-balanced meal. "If they do what I did, they'll be just fine," he says. "After all, I survived, didn't I?"

Okay, okay. But it's not just their eating habits I worry about. I don't know their friends. And unless they tell me about their activities, I don't know where they spend their free time—in the college dorm, hanging out with buddies in the common lounge, sipping soda at the local coffee shop, or none of the above. I hope they go to bed at a decent hour, but I can't ensure they sleep eight hours each night.

I also understand the angst that millions of mothers experience when they watch their teenagers climb behind the steering wheel of the family car to drive solo after earning their driver's licenses. *Will he remember to use his turn signals? Will she drive defensively?*

And each September, millions more experience the apprehension that arrives with the first day of school. Ah—I remember it well. *How will Matthew cope?* I wondered. *He's so quiet…will he socialize?* I'll tell you a secret: I cried at the mere thought of sending him into a classroom under a stranger's tutelage with 25 other children about whom I knew nothing. Matters worsened when, the day before school began, Matt looked up at me and announced, "I don't want you to drive me. I want to ride on the bus."

Gene came home from work at noon on Matt's first day of school, minutes before the bus arrived. Together we watched the vehicle door swing open. The yellow monster swallowed my baby and slammed its mouth shut.

Inside, Matthew found a seat, albeit without a seatbelt. *Such an ill-equipped vehicle can't be safe!* I thought. *There should be laws against such things!* The bus lurched and drove away.

Gene and I looked at each other. Our eyes betrayed our thoughts: *Should we? Yes!* We jumped into our car and shadowed the bus to school. We parked at the far end of the parking lot and watched from a distance until Matt disappeared into the classroom.

I cried all the way home. *God, please keep Matt safe. If he feels lonely or frightened, remind him that You're with him,* I prayed.

Twelve years later, I watched 18-year-old Matthew stride across our local airport's tarmac and board a plane that would carry him away for a two-year overseas missions commitment. This time I couldn't follow him. Would he find his connecting flights? Would his luggage arrive with him? More importantly, who would care for him if he got ill? Or who would reassure him if he grew homesick? A literal, physical ache filled my heart.

Reason to Fear

Humanly speaking, we have reasonable cause to fear for our kids' well-being. Today's society tempts and taunts them in every way imaginable. Television, videos, and computer games make illicit sex and violent behavior appear the norm. The Internet makes pornography readily accessible and invites evil-seekers into our homes. Biblical values are considered old-fashioned; those who respect them are labeled hatemongers.

We have no guarantees our kids will escape bumps and bruises or worse. I shudder when I hear of children being abducted from their own homes. Sometimes the perpetrators are relatives; sometimes they're neighbors or strangers.

The Columbine tragedy is forever etched in our memories. Who can erase the mental images of teenage students huddling and praying as two black-clad peers opened fire on human targets? And beyond North American borders, we'll always remember the innocent children from Beslan, Russia, who died in the terrorist attack on their school.

Thankfully, incidents of that magnitude are rare, but consider the dangers of everyday life. According to the National Center for Injury Prevention and Control, U.S. poison control centers handle an average of one poison exposure every 15 seconds. More than 90 percent happen in the home and involve the ingestion of cosmetics, plants, and housecleaning products. In 2000, more than 100,000 poisonings resulted in hospitalization.[1]

Here's another statistic. Emergency departments in the United States treat more than 200,000 children ages 14 and younger for playground-related injuries each year. In 1995, playground-related injuries among children ages 14 and younger cost an estimated $1.2 billion.[2]

My youngest child, Kimberly, accounted for one of those statistics. One sunny summer afternoon, I loaded my children and a friend's three kids into our van and drove to a nearby park so they could enjoy its new playground equipment. The kids joked and laughed as they climbed on the toys. But the fun ended when Kim tumbled five feet from a platform to the pea gravel below.

Kim whimpered as I turned her over and picked the gravel from her mouth. We returned home, but when her level of consciousness declined, I took her to a hospital emergency room. A CAT scan confirmed a concussion, and the doctor admitted her to the hospital for observation.

By early evening Kim was her usual perky self. My husband was reading her a bedtime story when our pastor dropped by to visit. As the men chatted, Kim played with the tray table. All was well until the pastor inadvertently reached over and lowered the tray, squishing Kim's little fingers! I don't know who hurt more—Kim or the pastor!

Accidents happen despite our best efforts to keep our kids safe. It's a miracle they survive until adulthood without wearing bubble wrap, knee pads, elbow pads, helmets, or steel armor. Our task would be far easier if children bore lights and sirens programmed to flash and wail whenever danger lurked.

We live in a world where bad things happen, but that's nothing new. Peek into history with me and meet another mother who feared for her child's safety, and for good reason.

History's Heroine

Prior to Moses' birth, Egypt held the Hebrew nation in slavery. Scripture says that the Egyptians were "ruthless with the Israelites, forcing them to make bricks and mortar and to work long hours in the fields" (Exodus 1:14). Despite the oppression, the Israelites multiplied and flourished. This unnerved the Egyptians.

The king feared that the Israelites would multiply, join the Egyptians' enemies, and eventually leave the country, so he announced a decree that struck terror into every mother's heart: He commanded the midwives to kill all baby boys at birth. Fortunately, the midwives feared God more than they feared Pharaoh and refused to play along with his diabolical scheme. When the king discovered the midwives' disobedience, he devised another plot. This time, he ordered his own people to throw every newborn Jewish boy into the river.

Slavery, a wicked king, and an evil edict—the combo provided ample justification for Hebrew moms to fear for their children's well-being. In this setting, however, we meet a mom named *Jochebed*. Put yourself in her sandals for a moment. Imagine giving birth to a baby boy at that time in history. Imagine trying to stifle your infant's cries, or trusting your other kids to keep silent about their tiny sibling, or juggling work with nursing your newborn—especially with a hate-filled supervisor scrutinizing your every move. On a stress-o-meter, you might max out! No celebrating your wee one's arrival with a beautifully decorated nursery. No birth announcement in the *Egyptian Times*. And no shower thrown by your girlfriends.

Jochebed's life was stress-filled all right, but this amazing mama disobeyed the law and hid her son at home for three months. When she could hide him no longer, she laid him in a wicker basket and placed him among the reeds on the bank of the Nile. That location brought its own dangers: the river's current, biting bugs, and cranky crocodiles.

Scripture doesn't say Jochebed was afraid, but we can use our sanctified imaginations and assume so. After all, what mother wouldn't be, considering the circumstances? Nevertheless, she faced her fear and proceeded with her plan.

Perhaps she asked a few what-ifs: *What if a wild animal attacks this basket? What if the weather turns ugly? What if an Egyptian discovers my baby?* Despite her misgivings, Jochebed moved forward. What was the secret to this woman's courage?

The Secret

I've discovered an important truth about facing fear as I've traveled this journey called motherhood. Author and speaker Carol Kent sums it up: "The solution to overcoming fear is not positive self-talk or a greater effort to control my own behavior or the behavior of others. The solution is a broken humility and trust in a sovereign, engaged, and loving God."[3]

Regardless of how hard I try, I cannot control my children, nor would I want to. God has wired them uniquely. He has a purpose for their lives. He wants to conform them to the image of Jesus Christ and to use their giftedness to build His kingdom on earth. I dare not stand in His way. Fulfilling His plans is His job; trusting Him and His methods for doing so is mine.

Just as I cannot control my kids, neither can I always control the circumstances that surround them. I simply can't be with them, hovering over them like a protective mother hen all day every day. That leaves me with one recourse—to follow Jochebed's example. To focus on God's ability to keep my children and then to release them into His care.

That sounds so simple, but I'd be lying if I said I've found it so. On the contrary, I've found it to be faith stretching and sometimes downright nerve-racking. Perhaps you've had a similar response.

Maybe you're a recently divorced mom fighting for custody of your children. You're doing everything possible to effect a positive outcome. *What if I lose?*

Perhaps you've just reentered the workforce and have placed your toddler in daycare. *What if my child catches a weird virus or learns another youngster's bad behavior?*

Maybe your child suffers from severe allergies, and you're concerned for his health while at school. *What if he eats something he shouldn't?*

We can easily focus on the what-ifs and get drawn into the whirlpool of uncertainty. When that happens, fear enslaves us. Our joy fizzles, and our courage wanes. The only way to escape the whirlpool is to grab the lifeline—the knowledge of who God is—and hold on tight.

We can either focus on the circumstances swirling around us and let fear pull us down, or we can recall the character of this faithful, sovereign, engaged, and loving God and find rest. The choice is ours.

Live Jitter Free

When we lived in Nepal, I saw people carry immense loads. I once saw a man bearing a 200-pound sack of sugar on his back. *A person isn't made to carry such a weight,* I thought. Regardless, the man had no other option. He lived several days' walk from the bazaar. No motor roads existed in that area of the country. He didn't own a horse or mule. If he wanted the sugar supply, he had to carry it himself.

Living in fear for our kids' well-being is like piggybacking a huge weight, one that we're not meant to carry. Unlike the Nepalese man, however, we have a choice because God has offered to carry our load for us. "Cast all your anxiety on him because he cares for you," says 1 Peter 5:7 (NIV).

We can continue our journey, stooped and hunched, and say, "Thanks, but no thanks. I'd rather bear the burden of my fear." Or we can respond by saying, "Thank You. Here are my worries. They're Yours."

The first response produces jitters. The latter promises joy. When we do what God tells us to do, the burden falls away. Freedom replaces bondage. And rest replaces the pain that comes from the anticipation of evil.

Cheryl understands this truth. I met her while speaking at a ladies' retreat in Washington state. I listened as she told me about her children.[4]

"I have three sons," she said. "Two are Marines. One is serving in Iraq for the second time since the war began. He's 21 years old. The other is 19 and in training. His wife is due to have their first child in a few weeks."

Words escaped me. I thought of my son at age 21 and tried to imagine how I'd feel if he was a Marine in Iraq. My imagination didn't want to go there.

Cheryl and her sons stayed in my thoughts long after the retreat ended, so I phoned her for an update. Colin, the eldest, had returned safely and had transferred to a unit that would not deploy again. The younger, Scott, was now the proud daddy of a beautiful baby boy. He'd finished training and started work.

On his second day, however, his commanding officer announced that he would be sent to Iraq within the month. "I'm just glad I won't have two boys there at the same time," said Cheryl. "One is difficult enough."

"How do you cope?" I asked.

"I belong to an online support group," said Cheryl. "It's good to be a part of a group that understands what you're going through. But over and over, when my fears overwhelm me, I read the Bible and pray." Then she read a prayer she'd written in her journal shortly after Colin was sent overseas the first time:

> *I come to Your presence, Father, to bow humbly before Your throne. I seek Your face, Lord, for in Your face there is love. And even though my heart aches right now and I am weary, Your love is extended to me. Thank You for Your grace and Your mercy. Thank You for allowing me to know You, especially through all the pain in life right now. I can rejoice because You are on Your throne. You hold the world together in Your hands. Your love is greater than life itself.*
>
> *Thank You, Father, for being with Colin. Thank You for watching over him and guiding him. Thank You for loving him more than I ever can.*
>
> *Father, I miss him so much, my heart hurts for him. To hear how he's struggling makes me come to You and ask for Your mercy to be bestowed upon him in this time. Give him favor with those he's with. Give him strength and courage. I also pray for Scott. Help him realize that You are his source of strength.*

I feel so alone sometimes. I need You to fill my emptiness with Your love. Only You can satisfy my longing and heal my heart. Show me, Father, how to love and trust when I don't feel I can. Show me how to live.

Wouldn't it be nice if we could simply erase situations that cause fear, deleting them as if they were e-mails in our inbox? That will never happen, but in the midst of them we can learn to rest. Cheryl's journal entry reveals the secret.

Cheryl chose to obey God's command to cast her anxieties upon Him. She told Him exactly how she felt—alone, empty, and hurt—and she expressed her needs to Him as her heavenly Father. But she didn't stop there.

Read Cheryl's prayer again. Do you see where she placed her focus? Smack on the character of God. She acknowledged His kingship. She praised Him for His love. She extolled His grace, mercy, and sovereignty. She was honest about her fears and worshipped God in the midst of them.

We moms will never outgrow our concern for our children's well-being, but we can be free from paralyzing fear. Cheryl's example shows that this is possible. Freedom comes from believing that God is who He says He is and that this all-powerful, all-knowing, all-loving God holds our kids in His hands. Let's take a look at another mom whose story reinforces this thought.

Hannah's Story

Meet Hannah, a mother whose story is recorded in the Old Testament. Unable to conceive, she cried to God to give her a child. He honored her request with a baby boy, Samuel. Imagine Hannah's excitement! No longer would she feel inferior to her peers and, worse yet, to her husband's other wife. But her story has one little twist.

When Hannah begged God for a child, she promised to give the child back for His service all the days of his life (1 Samuel 1:11). So after Samuel was weaned, Hannah took him to the temple and left him in the care of the priest Eli.

Leaving Samuel at the temple must have been tough enough for Hannah. In our camp ministry, I've seen mothers cry when they say goodbye to their kids for one week. Hannah would see her boy only once a year.

But leaving Samuel with Eli may have caused an added burden. You see, Eli didn't have a stellar reputation for raising great kids: "Now the sons of Eli were scoundrels who had no respect for the LORD or for their duties as priests" (1 Samuel 2:12-13).

If I'd been wearing Hannah's sandals, I might have been tempted to renege on my promise. But Hannah, amazing mommy that she was, placed her focus on the character of God and moved ahead. These are her words as she prepared to leave Samuel with Eli:

> My heart rejoices in the LORD!
>   Oh, how the LORD has blessed me!
> Now I have an answer for my enemies,
>   as I delight in your deliverance.
> No one is holy like the LORD!
>   There is no one besides you;
>   there is no Rock like our God.
> Stop acting so proud and haughty!
>   Don't speak with such arrogance!
> The LORD is a God who knows your deeds;
>   and he will judge you for what you have done.
> Those who were mighty are mighty no more;
>   and those who were weak are now strong.
> Those who were well fed are now starving;
>   and those who were starving are now full.
> The barren woman now has seven children;
>   but the woman with many children will have no more.
> The LORD brings both death and life;
>   he brings some down to the grave but raises others up.

The LORD makes one poor and another rich;
 he brings one down and lifts another up.
He lifts the poor from the dust—
 yes, from a pile of ashes!
He treats them like princes,
 placing them in seats of honor.
For all the earth is the LORD's,
 and he has set the world in order.
He will protect his godly ones,
 but the wicked will perish in darkness.
No one will succeed by strength alone.
 Those who fight against the LORD will be broken.
He thunders against them from heaven;
 the LORD judges throughout the earth.
He gives mighty strength to his king;
 he increases the might of his anointed one
(1 Samuel 2:1-10).

Hannah was quite the praying mom! Her words give no evidence of whining or self-pity or fear. Rather, they focus on God—His deliverance (verse 1), His holiness and uniqueness (verse 2), His knowledge and justice (verse 3), His power, sovereignty, and mercy (verses 6-8), His rule over the earth (verse 8), His protection (verse 9), His judgment (verse 10), and His ability to give strength (verse 10).

This historical heroine possessed a solid understanding of God's character. That knowledge gave her the courage to release Samuel into Eli's care and ultimately into God's care. The result? Samuel became one of Israel's greatest prophets.

Knowing God More Intimately

We often tell our kids, "God has a special purpose for your life." Truth is, He has a special purpose for moms too. Regardless of our age, race, or walk of life, He wants us to enjoy a relationship with Him. He wants us to know Him so well that we will trust Him

HOW CAN I HELP MY
CHILD DEAL WITH FEAR?

Kids have fears too. It's easy to dismiss them with a casual, "Don't be silly, everything will be all right," but doing so may leave them feeling unloved or lied to. Here are several practical suggestions to help calm their anxiety.

- Remind them of God's faithfulness to them in the past. Tell them stories from your own life. Read age-appropriate stories about heroes of the faith.

- Teach them to tell their fears to God and to praise Him for being bigger than anything they'll face.

- Memorize Scripture with them. Philippians 4:6 is a good one: "Don't worry about anything; instead, pray about everything. Tell God what you need, and thank him for all he has done."

- Model an attitude of trust. Let them hear you express confidence in God and His ways. Make sure your countenance and body language reinforce the same message!

---

implicitly. If we let fear become a friend, it can be a major player in accomplishing that purpose. I discovered that to be true when Stephanie was born.

The morning after the international airline refused my passage, our family of four plus Gene's mother, a British midwife, and a Nepalese driver climbed into a Land Rover. We bid tearful goodbyes to our coworkers and then bumped from pothole to pothole as we descended the winding road from the hospital to the main highway. Twelve hours later, dusty and exhausted, we arrived at a missionary guesthouse in Kathmandu.

The next morning my nightmare continued like a surreal scene from a never-ending movie. This time, the script involved saying goodbye to my three-day-old daughter. I nursed her one last time, caressing her tiny fingers and memorizing the shape of her lips. I cradled her, inhaling her powdery-fresh baby scent. *Is this the last time I'll see her alive?* I wondered. *O God, I'm afraid she'll die before I see her again.*

Gene's voice interrupted my thoughts: "It's time." Our midwife prayed for God to keep father and daughter safe enroute to Seattle. Moments later, Gene kissed me goodbye. He took Stephanie from me, wrapped her in a blanket, threw a diaper bag over his shoulder, and left the room. I stared at the door as it closed behind him, my thoughts reeling from the events that had broadsided us.

I rested on my bed for several hours, comforting a feverish and cranky Matthew. He cried for his daddy; I cried to my heavenly Father. *Lord, what are You doing? I don't understand the circumstances and, frankly, I don't like them. Why have You allowed this to happen? What are Your plans for this baby girl?*

Into one of the blackest moments of my life came a song:

> Great is Thy faithfulness, O God my Father,
> There is no shadow of turning with Thee;
> Thou changest not, Thy compassions, they fail not;
> As Thou hast been, Thou forever will be.
>
> Pardon for sin and a peace that endureth,
> Thine own dear presence to cheer and to guide;
> Strength for today and bright hope for tomorrow,
> Blessings all mine, with ten thousand beside!
>
> Great is Thy faithfulness! Great is Thy faithfulness!
> Morning by morning new mercies I see;
> All I have needed Thy hand hath provided;
> Great is Thy faithfulness, Lord, unto me![5]

THOMAS O. CHISHOLM, © HOPE PUBLISHING CO.

The lyrics washed through my mind, replacing my fear for Stephanie's physical well-being with courage and confidence in my heavenly Father. The song offered no guarantee that Stephanie would live or that she would lead a normal, productive life. But its words reminded me that come what may, God would prove Himself faithful. The lyrics promised strength for one day at a time, hope for tomorrow, and blessings beyond my wildest imagination. And they reassured me that God's presence would accompany me on my journey...a journey that, unknown to me at that moment, would lead my family through darker days ahead, days that would require more courage than we could muster on our own.

A week later, back in the States, we stood with a cardiologist outside our newborn's hospital room. "Stephanie has a heart defect," the doctor said. "She'll likely die within the month. If she lives to be two years old, she'll need open-heart surgery. Problem is, babies this sick rarely survive that long."

My gut wrenched and my knees threatened to buckle. *How much can a tiny baby endure?* I looked past the doctor into my daughter's glass-walled room. She was the only occupant—a safeguard against the possibility of spreading third-world viruses. A note attached to her incubator read, "Pregnant nurses are not to handle this baby."

Fear, like a raging river rolling and tumbling toward a Niagara-sized waterfall, threatened to push me over the brink. But God, in His goodness, threw me a lifeline: *Great is Thy faithfulness; great is Thy faithfulness.*

Once again the lyrics reminded me that regardless of what the future held, God would be true to His character. Focusing on Him and His promised faithfulness calmed my fears. I still felt concern for my baby's well-being, but the intensity of the "pain that arises from the anticipation of evil" subsided. In its place, I gained courage to walk through those hospital doors every morning, and I gained a peace that carried me through Stephanie's 11 subsequent surgeries and her bout with meningitis when she was less than a year old.

If I'd written the script, I would not have included Stephanie's medical emergencies. Heaven knows I prayed for healing from hydrocephalus and other concerns. Others did too. But God said no. Instead, He walked with us through the dark days and granted us a firsthand opportunity to experience Him as a God who provided strength for the challenges.

In the midst of frightening circumstances, we also experienced God as our provider. He supplied babysitters for Matthew so Gene and I could spend time with Steph at the hospital. He provided funds to pay for the medical bills. He gifted us with a church family who showered us with love and practical help. He even gave us a primary care doctor who had grown up in a third-world country and was sensitive to us as we experienced reentry culture shock.

Fear for my daughter's well-being could have been my undoing. Instead, it drove me to my knees and opened my eyes to see the beauty of who God really is. I've learned to trust this amazing God for Stephanie's future. She's 22 years old now and has graduated from Bible college. Her goal is to serve God overseas. She still needs her shunt, and I could stress over the what-ifs of possible medical emergencies. But why waste so much energy doing that when almighty God holds her in His hands?

Our Protector

More recently, an incident concerning Matthew helped us understand God as a protector. Earlier in this chapter, I mentioned that Matthew left home at age 18 to pursue a two-year overseas missionary opportunity. Believe me, letting him go wasn't easy. Well-meaning people asked me, "Aren't you scared? How can you let him travel alone, especially so soon after 9/11?"

I admit it, I felt fearful. But when I looked back to the ways God revealed Himself to us after Stephanie's birth, I found courage for this new challenge. Had God changed over the years? No. Did He still care for me? Yes. Did He still want me to cast my anxieties upon Him? Yes. I also clung to my conviction that God has a purpose for my kids' lives and that I have no right to stand in His way.

With these thoughts in mind, I released my son and entrusted him into God's care. At the end of the initial two years, Matt enrolled for a third. For those three years, he lived aboard an oceangoing ship with about 200 other young people from 40 nations. They ministered in ports throughout the Caribbean, Central and South America, and Africa.

On one occasion, while in Martinique, Matt and his girlfriend (now his wife, Cheryl) left the ship and strolled to a nearby park, where they sat on a bench and chatted. As they visited, a stranger approached. He began asking questions about the ship, and then he asked for money.

Matthew recognized signs of alcohol and drug abuse. Not wanting to contribute to the stranger's addiction, he said, "I don't think I can help you with that."

The man glared and replied, "I have a gun." He motioned with his hand, which was stuffed in his pocket.

Matthew didn't know whether to comply with the man's request or call his bluff, but he knew he had to act quickly. At that exact moment, Cheryl saw another man approaching. For some reason even Matt doesn't understand, he (Matt) hailed the passerby, who immediately joined the group. By that time, the would-be robber had pulled his hand from his pocket. He'd been telling the truth: He held a gun.

Any other passerby might have bolted at the sight of the gun. Not this guy. He planted himself between the weapon and the rookie missionaries and engaged the robber in conversation. His actions enabled the kids to escape. They'd run only a few seconds when they heard shouts. They looked back and saw the thief in hot pursuit, but the stranger had vanished. Fortunately our kids outran the robber and found safety aboard the ship.

Who was the second stranger? Where did he come from? What prompted him to risk his own life to save the lives of two foreigners? And how did he disappear so quickly?

Perhaps he was an angel, a French-speaking secret agent assigned to Martinique that afternoon. I can only guess. But I know one thing for certain—God protected Matthew and Cheryl in a way that I couldn't have. And Matthew knows it too. If he'd heard a gazillion sermons about God's sovereignty and protection over his life, he couldn't have been impacted more than seeing it up close and personal.

Where Was God When...?

Because Matthew and Cheryl experienced physical protection from a would-be robber that day in Martinique, I can easily proclaim God's goodness in their situation. Obviously, He was with them and kept them from harm. But what would I say if their situation had turned out differently?

Every day, children are injured in accidents, diagnosed with terminal illnesses, victimized by adults who should be protecting them, and even killed by evil people. Perhaps you've seen this up close. You did everything possible to protect your child, but still your worst fears came true. I wish I could reach beyond these pages and give you a long hug.

We live in a fallen world in which bad things happen, and sometimes they happen to our kids. Try as we might, we can never guarantee their safety, but we can guarantee that they are never beyond the realm of God's presence. Their lives are in His hands—the One who loves them more than we ever could and who has eternal purposes far beyond our comprehension. He simply asks us to trust Him.

If you haven't already, I pray you'll pour out your heart before God and expect to experience His strength, peace, and healing power. "The LORD is close to the brokenhearted; he rescues those who are crushed in spirit" (Psalm 34:18). He knows how you feel. He sent His Son into the world and then watched Him face danger, sufferings, and death. But the story didn't end when the soldiers sealed Christ's tomb.

Three days later, Christ rose from the dead! Death and defeat were vanquished for all who believe on His name. Regardless of what happens in this temporary life on earth, we have confidence that Christ Himself is with us and those we love, and we have hope.

Helpful Hints

Fear takes flight when we focus on God's character and His promises in the Word. But here are some other hints you may find helpful for your journey through motherhood.

Share your fears honestly with godly friends. Remember, you're not alone. Our circumstances might be different, but we all experience similar feelings and doubts. You'll find encouragement and glean insights from those who have walked the path before you.

Pray with other moms. When my kids were in elementary school, I joined a Moms In Touch International (MITI) prayer group. It became a lifeline of sorts, a place where I could confidentially share concerns about my kids and pray for them with other moms of like mind. Together we praised God for who He was, thanked Him for previous answers to our prayers, and presented Him with new requests using His Word as our guide. Besides teaching me to pray, this group provided sweet fellowship and friendship. Check the MITI website for a group near you (www.Momsintouch.org). In Canada, visit www.motherswhocare.org, a similar ministry affiliated with Campus Crusade for Christ, Canada.

Sometimes circumstances make it difficult to leave home to attend a weekly prayer group. If that's true for you, find a girlfriend who will pray over the phone with you.

Visualize your fears in your closed fists. Now open your fists, palms down, and pray, *God, I release my fear of* _____ (name it). Turn your hands face up and pray, *I receive Your promises to protect my children. I receive Your love. I receive Your wisdom.* Debbie, an itinerant minister's wife who raised her children while traveling year-round from church to church in an RV for nearly 30 years, told me about this technique. I've found it very helpful.

Connect with a ministry that's geared to moms. Here are a few suggestions:

- Mothers of Preschoolers (www.mops.org)
- Hearts at Home (www.hearts-at-home.org)

- Moms@Work (www.momsatwork.org)
- Proverbs 31 Ministries (www.proverbs31.gospelcom.net)

So, dear moms, the fear for our kids' well-being can be either a faith buster or a friend. I pray we'll choose the latter, for that perspective will draw us closer to God and give us a more intimate understanding of His character. And that's the only attitude that brings freedom.

✦ POINTS FOR PROGRESS ✦

1. What are your greatest fears regarding your children's well-being?

2. How can fear become your friend rather than your worst enemy?

3. How does focusing on God's character overcome fearful thoughts regarding your kids' well-being? What facet of His character encourages you most when you're fearful?

4. Read Psalm 121:2-4 (NIV):

> My help comes from the LORD,
>   the Maker of heaven and earth.
> He will not let your foot slip—
>   he who watches over you will not slumber;
> indeed, he who watches over Israel
>   will neither slumber nor sleep.

What assurance do you find in these words regarding God's care for you and those you love?

5. How have you seen God's faithfulness in your life? Recall these experiences with your children so they can see Him at work.

+ PROMISES TO PONDER +

I look up to the mountains—
    does my help come from there?
My help comes from the LORD,
    who made the heavens and the earth!
He will not let you stumble and fall;
    the one who watches over you will not sleep.
Indeed, he who watches over Israel
    never tires and never sleeps.
The LORD himself watches over you!
    The LORD stands beside you as your protective shade.
The sun will not hurt you by day,
    nor the moon at night.
The LORD keeps you from all evil
    and preserves your life.
The LORD keeps watch over you as you come and go,
    both now and forever (Psalm 121).

Study this Book of the Law continually. Meditate on it day and night so you may be sure to obey all that is written in it. Only then will you succeed. I command you—be strong and courageous! Do not be afraid or discouraged. For the LORD your God is with you wherever you go (Joshua 1:8-9).

And I am convinced that nothing can ever separate us from his love. Death can't, and life can't. The angels can't, and the demons can't. Our fears for today, our worries about tomorrow, and even the powers of hell can't keep God's love away. Whether we are high above the sky or in the deepest ocean, nothing in all creation will ever be able to separate us from the love of God that is revealed in Christ Jesus our Lord (Romans 8:38-39).

✦ PRAYING THE PROMISES ✦

Dear God, I praise You as the Maker of heaven and earth. Thank You for watching over my children without slumbering or sleeping. Thank You for standing beside them as their protective shade. The sun will not hurt them by day, nor the moon by night. Please watch over their lives and keep them from all evil. Keep watch over them as they come and go, from now until forever. Amen.

Father, thank You for being with my children wherever they go. Keep their hearts filled with Your words so that wherever You lead, they will find strength and courage. In Your promised presence, may they find freedom from fear and discouragement. Amen.

Father God, I praise You for being a God of love and revealing Yourself through Jesus Christ. Thank You for promising that nothing—absolutely nothing—can separate my children from Your love. Fears for today, worries for tomorrow, and even the powers of hell can't keep Your love away from them. Thank You for your encouraging words! Amen.

3

Don't Touch *My* Stuff!

Fear always springs from ignorance.

RALPH WALDO EMERSON

On November 17, 1999, Ann was meeting with a client in her print shop when the phone rang. It brought a message that forever changed her life. "Your house is on fire, and it's fully involved," said the caller, the captain of the local Coast Guard. His words hit Ann like a punch in her stomach. When she arrived at the scene minutes later, those feelings turned to disbelief.

The house, perched on a pint-sized rocky island, had been her family's haven for 24 years. Now a charred, flaming skeleton stood in its place. Her treasures—family photographs, the mandolin her grandfather had made and sent from Finland, her children's artwork, her kids' baby clothes she'd saved for her grandchildren—had been reduced to water-soaked ashes.

Shock threatened to engulf Ann. But as it did, a familiar Scripture verse filled her mind: "Do not fear, for I am with you; do not be dismayed, for I am your God. I will strengthen you and help you; I will uphold you with my righteous right hand" (Isaiah 41:10 NIV).

The house and everything in it is gone, thought Ann. *This is a huge loss, but we're safe. Our kids are safe. Fire can't steal the happy memories*

55

made here. We still have the things that really matter. And we're not alone—God knows our situation, and He is with us.

Indeed, He was. And He proved it.

Ann and her husband eventually walked around the smoldering embers and surveyed the damage. Finally, realizing they should break the news to their children before someone else did, they turned to leave. As they did, an object on the wharf railing caught Ann's attention.

"What's that?" she asked no one in particular. When she drew closer, she recognized it as a book's blackened remains. The title, scarcely visible, read *Count Your Blessings.*

Ann picked it up and showed it to her husband and the firefighters. "Did you place this book on the railing?" she asked one after another. But none had seen or touched it. "It must have floated into the air and then landed there on its way down," suggested one fellow.

How that book settled in the exact place where Ann would see it as she left the island remains a mystery. But one thing is sure—its message instantly cast a proper perspective on her situation, and Ann holds fast to that perspective today.[1]

Our blessings consist of more than the money we earn and the material possessions we own. We can enjoy those things and share them with others, but their presence guarantees neither success nor fulfillment. And despite what television and magazine ads want us to believe, they cannot provide security. One moment, they're there; the next moment, they're gone. *Poof!*

Still, we struggle with the issue of stuff. Of Christ's 38 parables, 17 refer to possessions. And Scripture refers to them 2172 times! "That's three times more than love, seven times more than prayer, and eight times more than belief," says Wesley Willmer, author of *God and Your Stuff.* "About 15 percent of God's Word deals with possessions—treasures hidden in a field, pearls, talents, pounds, stables, and so on. Obviously God understood that believers would find this a difficult area of their lives to turn over to Him."[2]

Basing our security in things that can vanish in a flash leads only to hardship. Their disappearance leaves us wrestling with anger, bitterness, and fear. But if we hold our belongings loosely and base our security in God, trusting in His promised presence and help, we experience freedom that cannot be shaken regardless of what happens. And that confidence is a blessing no one can steal.

Perhaps, like Ann, you've experienced the loss of material possessions through a tragic fire. Or an intruder invaded your home and helped himself to your goods. Maybe your hubby recently received a pink slip from his employer. Or unexpected medical expenses have blown your budget to bits.

Maybe your circumstances are different. Your belongings haven't been taken from you, but every month you struggle with the fear of not having enough.

Let me ask you a personal question. When faced with financial insecurity or the loss of your belongings, how do you respond? Do you let fear cause sleepless nights? Do you throw up your hands in frustration? Speak some not-so-nice words to nearby family members? (Been there, done that.) Or do you respond by saying, "God knows my situation, and He is with me"?

The latter response should be our goal. I know, I know—you may be thinking, *Yeah, right. That's for the super-spiritual club, of which I'm not a member because I can't afford to pay the dues.* But wait! Maintaining an attitude of trust and rest is easier said than done, but it *is* possible. How? By understanding the character of God and how it relates to the nitty-gritty of everyday life.

Introducing...Jehovah Jireh!

"Almost all new discoveries of God—all fresh revelations of His person, nature and character—are tied to some crisis, some intense human experience," says David Wilkerson.[3]

Wilkerson retells the story of Abraham and Isaac, and of God's command for father to sacrifice son. Time and testings had matured Abraham's faith. Life's trials had taught him to trust and obey God as the promise-keeping all-powerful One. Now he stood poised, knife in hand, prepared to slay his own son because God told him to. And then he saw the ram. A substitute sacrifice—just in the nick of time!

Caught by its horns in a thicket several feet from the altar where Isaac lay, the animal struggled to free itself, but its efforts proved vain. Abraham retrieved the woolly critter. He cut the ropes that held Isaac, wrestled the bleating beast onto the altar where his son lay minutes prior, and performed the sacrificial rituals.

As nerve-racking as this experience sounds, it gave Abraham fresh insight into God as a faithful provider in the midst of extreme circumstances. To commemorate what he'd seen and learned, he dubbed that place "The LORD Will Provide" (Genesis 22:14).

God provided for Abraham back then, and He'll do the same for us today when we're walking in obedience to Him. How can I be so sure? Because His names describe His nature. One of these names is *Jehovah Jireh,* meaning roughly, "God will see to it." It carries the connotation of provision—He will see to it that our needs are met.

Providing for His children is a responsibility that flows from who God is. In other words, seeing to it that our needs are met isn't simply something He does when He feels like it. He does so because doing otherwise would be contrary to His nature.

Understanding this truth helps us place our security in God rather than in money and material possessions, and it grants freedom from fear. We see this freedom evidenced in the life of a poor widow (Mark 12:41-44). Rewind 2000 years and you'll see what I mean.

The Not-So-Worried Widow

It's a busy day at the temple treasury. Crowds jostle toward the offering container, into which dues are placed. Rich folks toss in large sums, hoping others might notice their sizeable contributions.

In the midst of the hubbub, our story's heroine quietly approaches the container. The widow holds two small copper coins worth only a fraction of a penny. Her offering isn't much, but it's all she has. If anyone has reason to be afraid of not eating another meal or not paying her bills, she does. But Scripture mentions nothing of her feeling fearful. Instead, it shows her trust in Jehovah Jireh to meet her needs.

How did she gain such confidence? Perhaps she remembered the account of the Israelites' long-lasting shoes and clothing during their 40-year wilderness hike (Deuteronomy 29:5). Maybe she recalled the story of another widow—the one for whom God provided flour and oil after she used her last grocery basics to bake bread for the prophet Elijah despite her own impending starvation (1 Kings 17:9-16). Whatever enabled our widow-friend to trust God in the face of adversity, her example challenges us to do the same when the going gets tough.

Our natural tendency is to cling more ferociously to our stuff when we feel it being stripped away. We're like toddlers who clutch frayed security blankets and shout, "Mine!" In contrast, we ought to open our hands and say to the Lord, *It's Yours. Do with it as You please. I trust You to care for me.* The ability to do so comes only from resting in the knowledge of who God is.

According to Wilkerson, the name *Jehovah Jireh* carries another connotation that broadens our understanding of His nature as provider: "God is showing us." Wilkerson says that besides providing for our material needs, "our Lord will reveal to us everything we need to obey Him. He will see to it that we are provided with the power, strength and resolve to do whatever He commands."[4]

Jehovah Jireh provides everything we need to live life as He's designed it. Just as He sent a substitute sacrifice on Isaac's behalf, so He's provided a substitute sacrifice to pay the death penalty for our sins—Jesus Christ, His Son. And He's given us the Holy Spirit to teach, guide, and empower us to do whatever He assigns us to do. When we're walking in right relationship with Him, He gives wisdom, inner strength, contentment, and joy.

Regardless of our financial status, we can rest assured that Jehovah Jireh will meet us at our point of need in every area of our lives. After all, He promised:

> So don't worry about having enough food or drink or clothing. Why be like the pagans who are so deeply concerned about these things? Your heavenly Father already knows all your needs, and he will give you all you need from day to day if you live for him and make the Kingdom of God your primary concern (Matthew 6:31-33).

Sometimes, however, He asks us to step from our comfort zone so we can experience Him as Jehovah Jireh in new ways. That's a bit scary! Just ask Sophie—she knows all about it.

Sophie's Story

One morning I received an e-mail from Sophie, a young married woman living in Australia. Several weeks prior, she'd begun reading my book *10-Minute Time Outs for Busy Women.* The Holy Spirit had used its words to challenge her priorities. Here's how she described her situation: [5]

> For the last four years, I have been pushing myself to work very hard in a full-time job that I don't like, another part-time job, and a masters degree program. My husband and I are lucky enough to own a little home and have recently returned from a trip overseas.
>
> On my return, I felt tearful and burned-out. I knew that I couldn't return to my stressful schedule. I felt God calling me to calm down and "nestle." My mother bought me your book of short devotionals for busy women, and it encouraged my decision to slow down and allow God to control my life rather than be controlled by my drive

to earn money and prove my value. I've done a lot of soul searching and have decided to leave my full-time job. Instead, I'll take another part-time job while I study.

Leaving my well-paid position is scary, but I believe it is what I am called to do. I pray that I'll have more time to spend with God, listening to what He wants for my life. I'd like to value my husband and do more for him. I'd also like to apply myself to my studies and have children in the next year or two.

I'm still a bit scared, but I'm trusting Him every step of the way.

I rejoiced with Sophie that despite anxious thoughts, she was willing to do what she believed God was leading her to do, and I prayed that He would honor her obedience. I could relate to her uneasiness—I'd experienced the same on my own journey. But I also knew that if Jehovah Jireh was issuing a command, He would take responsibility to catch her if she took the plunge.

I e-mailed a response, encouraging Sophie to jump. When she replied, two sentences in particular revealed the depth of her struggle: "The only pressure I have to earn, earn, earn comes from myself. Worry and anxiety about the future have become my god, with working and earning more money being the only ways I know to relieve it."

Thankfully, Sophie identified fear as her captor, and she chose to fight back. Some folks thought she was crazy. "Why would you exchange job security for risky contract work with no sick leave?" they asked. Sophie let the criticism fall by the wayside. When her first contract job didn't prove as promising as she'd originally hoped and her anxiety increased, she refused to second-guess her decision. Instead, she spent more time with God. And she and her husband reprioritized their spending habits, decreasing expenses by becoming a one-car family.

Nine months later, Sophie wrote again. This time, her enthusiasm and energy fairly bounced off the page. Smiling at the joy and confidence her words conveyed, I read the list of benefits she'd experienced since leaping into the unknown:

- I have more time to learn about God through attending Bible studies and church.
- I have more time to spend with family, especially elderly grandmothers.
- I'm producing higher-quality work.
- I'm more loving toward my patients at the health clinic where I work.
- The outcomes with my patients have improved.
- I've developed a greater respect for my body and am caring for it through proper nutrition and regular exercise.

The list thrilled me, but more good news followed as she detailed lessons she learned about God's character:

> This experience has taught me about God's faithfulness. In the early days, when I worried about not having enough work, I reminded myself that He would never lead me this far to leave me! Doing so caused my confidence to grow.
>
> I've learned of God's power—even though I had financial obligations, He always provided me with enough work to sustain them. I don't even know how He did it!
>
> And I'm learning more about God's love. I don't have to do anything to earn it!

Isn't that the truth? Besides being a provider by nature, God is faithful. God is powerful. And God is love. As Sophie discovered, intense human experiences reveal His nature in new ways. And when we genuinely understand His character, fear takes flight.

Where's Your Heart?

Sophie's story illustrates the truth of Matthew 6:19-21:

> Don't store up treasures here on earth, where they can be eaten by moths and get rusty, and where thieves break in and steal. Store your treasures in heaven, where they will never become moth-eaten or rusty and where they will be safe from thieves. Wherever your treasure is, there your heart and thoughts will also be.

Did Sophie find quitting her job an easy thing to do? No. Her heart skipped a beat when she sensed the Holy Spirit's nudges to resign from her position. But she knew she could no longer allow perks and paychecks to rule over her. She longed for freedom and chose to obey, proving that she treasured eternal values more than temporary gain.

Rick Joyner says, "If we are going to be submitted to the kingdom of God and represent it, we must rule over things and not allow them to rule over us. Any wrong or excessive attachments that we have are an open door for the enemy, who will usually come through that door in the form of a fear."[6]

Let's pause for a moment and make it personal. Have you left any doors open for the enemy? If you're struggling with an excessive attachment to a monthly paycheck, your fancy home, fine furniture, or any other material possession, you'd best make an adjustment before the enemy gains entry and sets up residence in your heart and mind. He has one motive—to steal your freedom by filling your mind with fear. He wants you to believe that your security rests in the things you can touch and see rather than in the invisible God. Whatever you do, do *not* give him the satisfaction of holding you hostage.

Several years ago, the enemy tried to wrap chains of fear around me. It happened when God directed our family to move to postcard-perfect British Columbia. There we would volunteer for one year as interns at a year-round Christian camping ministry.

This was a dream come true for my husband and me. For nine years we'd prayed for the opportunity to pursue a camping ministry. Finally, it happened. We just *knew* in our hearts that God was leading us north, and although He hadn't promised an easy ride, He'd promised to be with us.

Fulfilling God's assignment meant facing the reality of financial insecurity. Although our housing would be supplied, we would not receive an income during the internship. If a full-time position opened at the camp during that year and we chose to accept it, we would fall into the category of faith-supported missionaries and be required to raise our family's financial support. This felt a little daunting, especially as we'd grown to depend on my husband's paycheck. But we accepted the challenge because we believed it was God-given.

Friends and family watched. Some questioned our sanity for giving up our home and a steady income. Perhaps they thought our critical-thinking skills were a few cents shy of a dollar! Some expressed envy at our willingness to take the plunge and pursue our passion. In all honesty, we were scared. But we knew that obeying God's call was not optional.

Six months prior to moving, a real estate agent posted a For Sale sign on our four-year-old custom-built lakefront house. Six months rolled by without success. Our only recourse was to offer it as a rental. That's when we began playing "Good news, bad news."

Good news: Three young military officers viewed the house two days before our moving van was scheduled to arrive.

Bad news: They said, "We'll take it if you leave a washer and dryer."

Good news: My in-laws dashed to a local department store's scratch-and-dent section and found a new set of appliances. The men signed the rental agreement. We wiped nervous sweat from our brows.

Bad news: The next day, our insurance company dropped us because it didn't want to cover a house with out-of-state landlords. More sweat.

Good news: At six o'clock on the evening prior to our moving van's arrival, we signed papers with a new insurance company.

And so it went. Before the sun rose on Sunday morning, we rumbled off the driveway, headed for one of the bumpiest but richest adventures of faith we'd experienced until then.

Believe me, when I say *richest,* I'm not referring to monetary gain. On the contrary. As a wife and homemaker, I faced days when I didn't have the resources to buy groceries. On the tenth day of each month, the camp secretary placed a financial statement in our mailbox. The information revealed the total amount of donations we would receive at the end of the month. I checked the mailbox five or six times until the statement arrived. Without realizing it, I'd fallen into the trap of depending on human resources rather than on my heavenly Father's care.

Fear threatened me, and I waved the white flag of surrender. *God, did we make a mistake? Are we doing something wrong? Help us, please.*

And He did.

I'll always remember the Sunday afternoon when friends arrived carrying sacks filled with food. "God told us you needed this," they said. There was no other explanation—we hadn't breathed a word to anyone but the Lord.

I'll always remember when donations appeared from unexpected sources, enabling me to attend my first writers' conference.

And when a friend gave us boxes of hand-me-down clothes. Some items bore well-known name brands, and there was something for each family member.

And when someone handed us a check for $500 to pay for new tires for the car.

And when donations allowed our three children to participate in their school's band trips and various cross-cultural missions trips.

The list goes on and on. Each example defies math and human logic, and each stands as a testimony to Jehovah Jireh's involvement in His children's lives. Our journey has been filled with tests of our faith, and we're wealthier for them. Through them, I've learned to release excessive attachments to the things I can see and touch and to place my security in the almighty, invisible God instead.

So let me ask you a question, my dear sister. Where's your heart today? Is it stashed in a bank vault, protected under lock and key? Is it hidden in a jewelry box with Grandma's heirloom brooch? Is it crammed in your purse beside a half dozen or more credit cards? I hope not, because it won't last long in those places. Rust and moths and thieves are known for doing major damage.

There's only one honest-to-goodness safe home for your heart— in the hand of Jehovah Jireh, the One who sees to it that your needs are met.

Radical Lifestyle

One day I told a friend about our faith-tests and how they'd helped us understand God as Jehovah Jireh. He shook his head and said, "I earn $90,000 annually. I'd need either brain surgery or a heart transplant to live as you do." I told him that I wouldn't recommend our lifestyle unless it's clearly God-directed.

God calls His kids into a variety of kingdom-building roles. Some teach school. Others operate as CEOs of billion-dollar businesses. Some provide medical care for the world's poorest, while others use their homes to serve His purposes for their families and neighbors. Situations vary, and so do bank accounts.

But for Christ's followers, this factor remains constant: We have been bought with the blood of Jesus Christ; therefore, we belong to Him. So does our stuff. And He has the authority to do whatever He wants with it. Keeping our belongings in an open hand calls us to a radical lifestyle unfamiliar to today's world.

Society says we ought to demand our rights, stand up for ourselves, look out for number one. But Scripture says that we've been bought with a high price, so we are now Christ's slaves (1 Corinthians 7:22-23). What exactly does that mean?

Nelson's Bible Dictionary defines *slave* as "a person bound in servitude to another human being as an instrument of labor; one who has lost his liberty and has no rights." In simple terms, the Master owns it all—our bodies, our time, our paycheck, and everything in between. Paul, the greatest missionary in history, understood this concept. He called himself a slave of Christ Jesus, chosen by God to be an apostle and sent out to preach the Good News (Romans 1:1).

Unfortunately, the term *slave* irritates some folks.

> Not all believers are bondservants. Many come to an understanding of the sacrifice of Jesus for their sins, but they still go on living their lives for themselves. We were the slaves of sin and the cross purchased us, so if we are Christ's we are no longer our own, we belong to Him. A bondservant does not live for himself, but for his master. This commitment is not just an intellectual agreement with certain biblical principles—it is the commitment to a radical lifestyle of obedience.
>
> A bondservant does not have any money of his own, so he cannot spend freely what he has been entrusted with because it is not his. His time and even the family of a bondservant belong to his master.[7]

Perhaps some folks disagree with the slave teaching because fear rattles them. They want to maintain control over their possessions rather than relinquish them to a God they can't see. They'd prefer living within their comfort zone rather than stepping into the wide unknown. Fear looms large and overshadows faith.

Meet Sandra and Rob Pattison, a couple whose lifestyle is radical, all right. In 1992, God nudged them to start a portable soup kitchen for low-income neighborhoods in Nova Scotia, Canada.

"In my wildest dreams, I couldn't have imagined doing this," says Sandra, who cooks approximately 50 quarts of soup every week. "I'm not a kitchen whiz. If someone had told me what God had planned for us, I would have said, 'You have the wrong people.' But when God calls, He provides what's needed to get the job done."

When the Pattisons said yes to God, they had no financial support or savings account. They had two children, a mortgage, a car payment, and miscellaneous bills, but they also had confidence that God had given marching orders.

The day after Rob quit his job, God provided their first month's salary through the sale of their piano. When a newspaper article featured the Pattisons' venture, farmers began donating vegetables. People gave supplies to renovate a bus. When $5000 was required to buy a furnace and hot water heater for the vehicle, one man delivered a check for the full amount.

On another occasion, when the Pattisons had zero funds, a stranger phoned and said she wanted to make a donation. She suggested a meeting place about 30 minutes away. Rob hesitated at first, thinking she might donate $25—a sum not worth the gas and time the trip would require. But he went, and his doubts disappeared when the woman wrote a check for $5000.

In retrospect, Rob says starting this project wasn't rational, based on human standards. But he says he and Sandra felt a definite peace. "God gave us the faith to trust Him," he says. "Without it, we would have been scared to death. We recall sometimes how family and friends thought we were crazy—I can't blame them! I would have thought the same thing.

"We're human, though," he continues. "There have been times when we were down to our last penny, and we've battled doubt. We get a little concerned, but God has never failed us."

"I've learned lessons of faith I wouldn't have learned otherwise," adds Sandra. "We've witnessed miraculous answers to prayer that remind us how awesome and faithful God is. He has worked in so many practical ways, bringing necessary details together. I stand in awe."

Rob quotes Philippians 4:19 (NIV): "'And my God will meet all your needs according to his glorious riches in Christ Jesus.' We have the incredible privilege of seeing God do this on a daily basis," he says. "He's paid every bill and met every need. The past ten years have been incredible."[8]

Radical? Yes!

Easy? No!

But they're doing it for the Master, the One who bought them with a price more costly than all the wealth on earth. Check out their website at www.street.ns.ca.

Wise Stewards

Being called to a radical lifestyle of obedience doesn't give us the liberty to be foolish with possessions and then expect God to rush to our rescue when we encounter difficulties. If that's our attitude, we have every reason to be afraid, says Ellie Kay, American's family financial expert and author of *Half-Price Living*.

"My greatest fear when it comes to finances is that I won't be a good steward," says Ellie. "I ought to be afraid if I find myself outside God's favor by spending foolishly and not tithing."[9]

Ellie's passion is to see families experience financial freedom. She knows what it's like to face overwhelming consumer debt. She also knows how to overcome its stronghold, and she gladly shares her expertise—learned the hard way—with women internationally.

When Ellie married, her husband, Bob, brought into their union two daughters, $40,000 of consumer debt, and the conviction that God was directing him to join the Air Force. Following that pursuit meant a $15,000 decrease in annual income. Those digits looked daunting on paper, but other factors made their situation appear even more dismal: The births of five babies in seven years meant added expenses. Child support claimed one third of Bob's income. Taxes claimed another third. They tithed one tenth of his gross income. The couple lived off approximately 23 percent of his earnings.

Sounds grim, doesn't it? But get this! They were debt-free within two and a half years. What made this possible? God's supernatural provision and a hefty dose of wise stewardship.

We can never outguess God's methods of providing for His children. In Ellie's case, He cast her on the television program *The Price Is Right.* One of her prizes was a holiday travel trailer, which she promptly sold and applied toward her family's consumer debt. But such exciting events were not the norm. The norm meant finding creative ways to curb expenses and save money. In other words, Bob and Ellie practiced wise stewardship.

Some of us wince at the thought. The principle works for mathematical wizards, but not for the numerically challenged. Why, the mere thought of balancing the family checkbook gives us wrinkles and turns our hair gray! But wait—there's hope!

For those of us who feel incapable of managing household money matters, Ellie suggests that we take baby steps. We can begin by becoming masters of those financial matters closest to us. For instance, we can learn the value of clipping coupons and of shopping for quality used (or new!) items at garage sales and thrift stores. We can become savvy about saving money in other areas such as transportation, housing, entertainment, and insurance. And we can develop the discipline of tithing—giving God a portion of what belongs to Him in the first place. Once we've gained a measure of confidence in managing those financial areas, we can expand bit by bit.

"There are lots of resources to help women learn to manage the household budget in an easy step-by-step method," says Ellie. She suggests using computer programs such as Quicken or Microsoft Money. These programs outline all the necessary details and take the dread out of keeping financial records. Another helpful resource is www.crown.org, a website that features free online support.

Ellie offers yet another necessary piece of advice:

When it comes to stepping out in faith in various financial areas, whether it's quitting a job and coming home or venturing out to establish a small business, it's important to pray your way through it, but it's also important to be practical. Follow Luke 14:28—be wise and count the cost before you build the tower.

Work through the finances. Reorganize the budget. Determine where you can save money—perhaps by downsizing the house or number of vehicles. Sit down and put it all on paper. The numbers might not add up, but if you and your spouse agree that God is leading you to step out in faith, take that step and watch God meet you where you are. If it's God's will, it's His bill.

Perhaps God is nudging you toward a lifestyle change that will impact your money matters. Maybe you lack confidence in managing your family's finances. Maybe you're swamped with consumer debt as Ellie was, and fear is holding you hostage.

If so, God wants to set you free. *Trust Me,* He whispers. He extends His hand and beckons you to accept His invitation. Go for it! Accept His invitation. Do you know what will happen? You'll have the privilege of experiencing Him as your provider.

However, if unwise spending habits have put you in a financial pit, accepting His invitation means changing your direction. Breaking harmful habits can be scary too, but God is on your side.

Remember, "I am holding you by your right hand—I, the LORD your God. And I say to you, 'Do not be afraid. I am here to help you'" (Isaiah 41:13).

Cash Idol

When we lived in Nepal, we saw people worship idols every day. Sometimes our neighbors decorated stones with flower petals or red powder. Sometimes they offered coins or plates heaped with cooked rice to the rocks. They spent their affections on these stone gods from whom they sought help to deal with life's challenges. The scenes transported me to Old Testament days. Scriptural warnings about the follies of idol worship took on new meaning for me.

I don't see many blatant examples of that kind of idol worship in North America. But idolatry exists, albeit in a more subtle form. In our culture, we worship stuff: dollars and cents. Fast cars, fancy homes, and nice furniture. Stylish clothes and expensive vacations. We pour our affections, time, and energy into the things we can see and touch. In return, we hope to gain security. And this we do against the warnings of Jehovah Jireh, the invisible God who commands us not to fear because He'll see to it that our needs are met.

God wants to be our sole source of security. If other gods replace Him, sooner or later we discover that trusting in money and possessions yields only emptiness and pain. "For the love of money is at the root of all kinds of evil. And some people, craving money, have wandered from the faith and pierced themselves with many sorrows" (1 Timothy 6:10).

Sometimes we realize our folly. Sometimes we don't, so we try harder to fill the void with more possessions. But that means spending more money. At the end of the month, the bills arrive, and then we're forced to work harder and longer to pay them. We pierce ourselves with a consumer debt load that God never meant us to carry.

TOP-TEN GROCERY SAVINGS TIPS

These tips come courtesy of Ellie Kay—the money-saving guru. They'll help you ease financial worries in practical ways.

- Make sure the price is right. Buy quality but pay the least possible price.

- Hungry? Stay home! Shopping when you're hungry will tempt you to buy unneeded products. And leave your starvin' kiddies with a friend or your spouse so they can't con you into buying junk food.

- Try to buy items on sale and stock up.

- Become a coupon queen. Find out which stores offer double or triple coupons and use those coupons to buy sale items.

- Clip every coupon—for a swap box! Use a shoebox-size container to organize coupons at your workplace, club, or church. Fill a ziplock baggie with coupons and enclose a blank piece of paper called a name card. Write your name on the paper so you'll know you donated that particular bag. Each time you take a coupon from a particular bag, sign the name card. At the end of each month, a coupon coordinator removes the expired coupons and mails them to overseas military units. There, the coupons will be valid for an additional six months past the expiration dates.

- Sharing—the gift that keeps on giving! Clip coupons and use them to purchase sale items. Sometimes, if you use double coupons, you can get the item for free. If you can't use that item, donate it to a nonprofit organization.

- Get a tax deduction for sharing! Ellie says that on a $200 per month food budget, her family donated $1000 worth of groceries to the needy. Nonprofit organizations will issue receipts for tax-deductible gifts.

- Search high and low for bargains. Grocery stores often place pricey items at eye level. Check the upper and lower shelves for the good deals.

- Use a list—don't leave home without it! Taking your grocery list prevents you from buying on impulse, limits the amount of time you spend in the store, and keeps you on target.

- Check out the checkout! Ellie says that checkout clerks will overcharge the average customer as much as 18 percent in their lifetime. Make sure clerks scan items properly and give the correct coupon deductions.[10]

For more tips and information about Ellie's books, visit her website at www.elliekay.com.

According to Money-zine.com, the latest statistics from the Federal Reserve say that the United States' consumer debt of approximately $2.2 trillion works out to roughly $7400 of debt for every man, woman, and child in the nation. Nearly one in every 50 households in the States filed for bankruptcy in 2005. Ladies, I think we have a problem!

I've been pondering the debt dilemma for a while. From my observations, I propose four possible reasons why people fall into this trap.

1. *Impulsive shopping habits.* We see, we want, we buy. Charge it to a credit card and pay for it later.

2. *Failure to discern the will of God.* We *think* we know what He wants for our lives, so we pursue our plans but ignore the caution signs along the way. For example, Ellie Kay often speaks to Christian young people who are attending expensive Christian universities because they feel convinced that God has led them that direction. Trouble is, they have no money to pay the bills. By graduation day, they're owing $80,000 in student loans. If they marry a classmate who has done the same thing, they owe $160,000, and they're riddled with debt for the rest of their lives.

We must learn to differentiate between faith and presumption. If God truly leads us in a certain direction, then He *will* provide, even though He often comes through at the midnight hour. Prayer, reading the Word, practicing patience, and seeking the counsel of godly men and women will help us know whether we're walking on a faith journey or we've deceived ourselves into believing that our plans are God's will.

3. *Desire for acceptance, also known as the fear of rejection.* This is a big deal for many women, one that often leads us down the wrong path. We buy a house we can't afford because we crave the status of a particular neighborhood, or we buy clothes we don't need because we want to impress. When relationships disappoint, we try to fill our emotional hole with goods, but overboard spending leads to debt or worse yet, bankruptcy.

Karen O'Connor, author of *Addicted to Shopping,* says it like this: "Debt is not really a money issue. It is an issue of self-worth and our feelings of not being enough." She says every woman she knows who has major consumer debt struggles with a poor self-image. She says that the only way to wellness is first to surrender one's will to God and then to plan and take practical steps to pay off the debt.[11]

4. *Unbelief.* This also results from fear—the fear that God isn't big enough to look after us properly. In reality, the problem has nothing to do with God—He's more than capable. The trouble lies in our faulty understanding of who He is. And without a correct understanding of who God is, we become captivated by fear. We enlist our own human methods to meet life's challenges and uncertainties rather than wait for God to meet us where we are. Like our Nepalese neighbors, we bow to the things we can see and touch rather than to the almighty, invisible God.

If you're burdened by debt, ask the Holy Spirit to show you the root reason. Have you replaced God with the cash idol? Have you pursued your own plans, assuming they were God's? Are you fearful of rejection? Are you a captive of unbelief and afraid to surrender your well-being to the invisible God? Whatever the reason for your bondage, God wants to set you free. He wants us to lead rich lives regardless of what our bank accounts contain. True wealth comes from knowing and experiencing Him. True joy results from living life according to His Word. And true freedom flows from resting in His care. The more we understand His ability to provide everything we need, the greater our spiritual wealth.

✦ POINTS FOR PROGRESS ✦

1. "Almost all new discoveries of God—all fresh revelations of His person, nature and character—are tied to some crisis, some intense human experience," says David

Wilkerson. What intense human experience have you faced?

2. What new understanding of God did you discover through it?

3. Recall an instance when you faced financial insecurity or the loss of your material possessions. Did the enemy sneak fear into your life? If so, how did you deal with it?

4. Have you seen God provide supernaturally for your family or someone else? If so, what did He do?

5. What scares you the most about financial issues? What practical steps can you take to face these fears?

✦ PROMISES TO PONDER ✦

Sing out your thanks to the LORD;
  sing praises to our God, accompanied by harps.
He covers the heavens with clouds,
  provides rain for the earth,
  and makes the green grass grow in mountain pastures.
He feeds the wild animals,
  and the young ravens cry to him for food.
The strength of a horse does not impress him;
  how puny in his sight is the strength of a man.
Rather the LORD's delight is in those who honor him,
  those who put their hope in his unfailing love
(Psalm 147:7-11).

Taste and see that the LORD is good.
  Oh, the joys of those who trust in him!
Let the LORD's people show him reverence,
  for those who honor him will have all they need.
Even strong young lions sometimes go hungry,

but those who trust in the LORD will never lack any
good thing (Psalm 34:8-10).

For the LORD God is our light and protector.
   He gives us grace and glory.
No good thing will the LORD withhold
   from those who do what is right.
O LORD Almighty,
   happy are those who trust in you
(Psalm 84:11-12).

✦ PRAYING THE PROMISES ✦

*Heavenly Father, You alone are able to provide for creation's
needs. Thank You for doing it so faithfully. Help me trust
You as simply as the wild animals and birds do. Teach me
to honor You and to place my hope in Your unfailing love.
Amen.*

*Dear Lord, I praise You because You are good. Align my
heart to trust You and show You reverence. As You do, I
will trust You to supply what I need and to see to it that I
will never lack any good thing. Amen.*

*Dear God, I praise You for being my light and protector.
When fear threatens to overwhelm me, please remind me
that You will withhold no good thing from me if I do what
is right. Thank You for promising happiness to me if I trust
in You. Amen.*

4

Lessons Learned
in the Storm

*I am not afraid of storms, for I am
learning how to sail my ship.*

Louisa May Alcott

"Stay with us, Jan," whispered a nurse aboard the medevac heli-copter as it pounded through the night sky over Minneapolis, Minnesota. "We're almost there." Far below, the city's twinkling lights cast a serene scene—a stark contrast to the scenario aboard the chopper, where thirty-year-old Jan Turner fought for her life.

Jan was the single mother of adopted boys ages four and ten, a Christian school teacher, and a music minister. Earlier that day—November 6, 1989—she'd led congregational singing as usual at her church's Sunday morning service. But that morning Jan felt faint. She left the service early, returned home, and crawled into bed.

Within hours, Jan began drifting in and out of consciousness. Her temperature soared. Her blood pressure plunged. Her father raced her to the local hospital's emergency room, where doctors diagnosed her with pneumococcal pneumonia. They summoned a medevac helicopter for transport to a better-equipped facility but questioned whether she would survive the trip.

Thirty-five minutes after takeoff, the helicopter landed at Abbott Northwestern Hospital. Medical personnel flew into action, wheeling Jan from the chopper to the intensive care unit.

Jan's spleen had been removed when she was a college student. Without it now, infection coursed through her bloodstream. She lapsed into a coma and hovered between life and death. A respirator breathed for her. Doctors administered kidney dialysis and blood transfusions. Finally they gathered Jan's father, sister, and brother to discuss her condition.

The medical professionals expressed their doubts that Jan would survive. They told her family that even if she did, they feared for her quality of life. They suggested the possibility of discontinuing life support, but Jan's family disagreed. Instead, they sat by her bedside, praying and playing praise and worship music day and night. A few days later their decision paid off.

Jan shocked medical personnel when, after more than a week, she woke from her coma knowing her identity and location. She asked questions about her children and what she'd experienced medically during her coma. She studied her blackened, curled fingers and asked an intern, "What are you going to do about my hands?" Because blankets covered her feet, she didn't realize that they too were black.

Tears filled the intern's eyes. She answered, "I'm sorry, Jan. There's nothing we can do." She paused for a moment. And then she spoke words that unleashed a storm like no other Jan had ever experienced.

"Your body struggled to survive by pushing its blood to your main organs. This caused your extremities to develop gangrene. Your hands and feet will be amputated if you consent."[1]

Sink or Sail?

Stay with me—that's not the end of Jan's story! I'll tell you the rest in a moment, but first I want to interject a truth that can make or break us.

As Jan discovered and you may have already experienced, life can change in a nanosecond. One minute the sky's blue. The weather's balmy. But in an instant—without warning and through no fault of your own—black clouds roll in and dump on you…

- A phone call jars you from a deep sleep: "Your teen has been in a serious accident. Come to the hospital immediately."

- Your routine medical exam yields abnormal results. The doctor has ordered further tests.

- Your daughter spills her secret. She's pregnant and has made an appointment to abort your grandchild.

- Your son spills *his* secret—he's gay. And he's HIV positive.

- Your husband admits to having an affair with a coworker, and now he's contemplating divorce.

- You're moving across the country, leaving friends and familiarity behind.

- Your senior parent is ailing and requires constant care. The responsibility is yours.

- You've already pared your family's budget to a bare minimum. And now you've been laid off work.

Whatever the circumstances, personal storms bring sudden howling winds strong enough to snap trees, knock out power, and even snuff out life. Gentle ripples become wild whitecapped waves. The little boats in which we sit rock and reel and threaten to capsize.

There's no doubt about it—storms are scary. Within seconds of striking, they can leave a path of devastation in their wake. And we're left facing a decision of paramount importance—how will we respond?

Some folks shake their fists at God and curse His name for

the lousy weather that's ruined their day—or their lives. Bitterness invades their souls, plants a scowl on their faces, steals their joy, and injures their relationships with other people.

Some retreat into silence and solitude, either unable or unwilling to share their pain with anyone. Fear of losing control or of facing an uncertain future sometimes drives them to desperate measures.

Others succumb to paralyzing fear. They can't sleep, can't eat, and can't think rationally enough to take the next step because what-ifs hold them captive. *What if I make the wrong decision? What if life never returns to normal as I know it? What if the situation turns from bad to worse? What if I can't cope?* Fear tells them that the crisis has rendered them helpless, and they believe it.

And then we find those who, in the midst of fear or utter despair, choose to fall on their knees before God and cry for help. They cling to Him and His promises like shipwrecked souls cling to life preservers in the midst of a midnight storm at sea.

Jan Turner was one of those souls. She had accepted Jesus Christ as her personal Savior at a Christian summer camp while in fourth grade. Bible reading, prayer, and fellowship with other believers had strengthened that relationship. Throughout college, she'd participated in music ministry and evangelism. As an adult, she'd pursued vocational Christian service. She understood the importance of depending on God's strength day by day. But now, facing quadruple amputation and listening to a doctor explain how to use prosthetics, Jan realized afresh her absolute dependence on God for strength.

Delving into the Bible for encouragement, she read, "For I can do everything with the help of Christ who gives me the strength I need" (Philippians 4:13). She seized that promise and hung on for dear life. *Dear Lord,* she prayed, *with Your perfect strength, a full and productive life will become my reality.*

When the demands of her rehabilitative therapy exhausted her, she goaded herself on with Romans 8:37: "Despite all these things, overwhelming victory is ours through Christ, who loved us." Again, she chose to believe God's promise. She personalized the verse by saying, *Jan Turner, you're more than a conqueror because of what Christ did for you on Calvary.*

Jan refused to let the storm knock her flat. Instead, she embraced it as a catalyst for understanding God's character more intimately. Through it, she discovered a fresh revelation of His enabling strength in the midst of extreme adverse circumstances. After surgeries and months of physical and occupational therapy, she mastered life skills that able-bodied people take for granted—cooking, eating, driving, and walking. She also earned a second degree in speech and communications and became an ordained pastor.

Jan often refers to her physical appearance when she tells her story. She explains that she looks different from most people on the outside, but she's the same on the inside. "I'm not disabled," she says. "I'm differently abled. The prefix *dis* means *not.* If I call myself disabled, I'm saying I'm not able. That's untrue. I *am* able. The Bible says I can do all things through Christ who gives me strength—He gives us things to do and empowers us to do them."

I admire Jan's attitude! She survived a tsunami of proportions that make my life's difficulties resemble a toddler's birthday party. She faced a storm that might have caused others to shrivel in fear, and she emerged a confident and joy-filled woman.

Her audiences laugh as she lists the benefits of wearing prosthetics. "I only change my socks a couple times a year," she says. "I can remove a casserole dish from a hot oven without using potholders. If we're cooking dinner over a fire, I can stoke the coals. I have two built-in hammers. Hey—I can pull wood ticks off my dog, give 'em a good squeeze, and they never know what hit 'em! I was five-four before I lost my legs. Now I'm five-eight. Through my experience, I've grown in more ways than one!"

Chances are slim that we'll grow in the same way as Jan, but we're guaranteed one thing. As long as we're warm and breathing, we'll face personal storms. We don't know when they'll strike or what they'll look like. But when they come, there will be no escaping their fury. They can either sink us or fill our sails and propel us forward along our journey. Which will it be?

The choice is ours.

Moving Beyond Fear

Bruce Larson offers some perspective:

> There is no way to live without fear. Nevertheless, it is possible to live beyond fear. Even those of us who have faith and who trust in God are going to find ourselves in scary situations. We need to learn to appropriate for our lives the reassurance of those words the Lord repeats so often in the Gospels, "Don't be afraid. Fear not."[2]

I agree with Bruce's words. When scary situations come my way, my initial response is often fear. My heart pounds and my thoughts bing-bang in every direction, concocting every possible negative outcome. That's when I'm faced with a choice: to allow fright to consume and control me, or do as God says and "fear not."

The latter is best by far. Rather than struggling with anxiety, sleeplessness, and stomach ulcers, I enjoy peace that bad news can't rattle. I'm able to obey God even though His ways make no sense to me. How is that possible when circumstances seem out of control? By focusing on God's character and believing that His promises are true.

My husband grew up in Washington state and spent lazy summer days at his family's waterfront cabin. When he entered junior high school, his folks built a permanent home on the beach. Waterskiing and sailing became regular activities.

While Gene splashed, rowed, paddled, and tacked, I was growing up on the Alberta plains. The nearest body of water, besides the chlorinated community swimming pool, was a man-made lake ten miles south of town. Several times each summer, my older sister and I jumped on our bikes and pedaled the 20-mile round-trip across the bald prairie. Sunburn and sweat were small prices to pay for the pleasure of floating on air mattresses and tanning on the sandy beach.

Gene and I met at a summer camp on an island in British Columbia. I took one look at his water-related skills and knew we were in different leagues. He taught me to ski and took me sailing, but my comfort level on the water lagged a few miles behind his. It still does.

True sailors, like my husband, embrace wind as the key that enables them to do what they love to do. They know their boats, and they know how to use the wind to their advantage. Landlubbers, on the other hand, hunker down and hold on for dear life.

I'll admit I've hunkered a few times. On one occasion, gale-force winds blew in suddenly while we were sailing around Quadra Island. Whitecapped waves slapped the 25-foot boat and sloshed over its sides. The vessel heeled on a 45-degree angle, enough to shove the cabin windows under the water's surface and turn my face a nameless shade of green.

Gene studied the water for ripples that revealed approaching gusts. He handled the tiller and adjusted the sails accordingly. And he wore a grin a mile wide. "Don't worry," he said. "Sailboats are made to do exactly what we're doing. Everything will be fine."

That's easy for you to say, I thought. I watched the waves roll and crash, and sheer terror filled my mind. *What if we capsize? What if someone falls overboard and drowns? What if that someone is me? I don't even like cold showers! H-e-l-p!*

I cowered in the corner of the cockpit, threatened by the storm and terrified of its potential effect. And that's when I heard a quiet voice say, *Don't be afraid. Be still and know that I am God.*

Whitecaps continued slapping the sailboat and soaking me with their spray, but my focus changed. Thoughts of a different storm, a different boat, and a different crew popped into my mind, and I recalled similar words spoken to a handful of fear-filled men more than 2000 years ago…

I Am Here

Jesus and His disciples had labored through another busy day. He wanted solitude, some quiet time alone with His Father to refresh and commune. At His command, the disciples left Him on shore, climbed into a boat, and headed across the lake. Several hours later, a storm swept in and caught the dozen in the dinghy off guard (Matthew 14:22-33).

Waves rolled and crashed and broke. The boat bounced and tossed. The disciples' stomachs churned. Their nerves grew tense. And just when they thought they couldn't handle any more, they spied a spooky specter, or so they thought, approaching them through the spray and mist. Their fear cranked up another notch, and they screamed in terror.

At the moment they thought their doom was sealed, they heard Jesus' voice: "It's all right. I am here! Don't be afraid." His words offered a calming reassurance of His presence, like those whispered by a mother who rushes to her frightened toddler's bedside at night: "Mommy's here. Don't be afraid."

But Jesus' words, "I am here," implied much more than a simple assurance of His presence. They conveyed the powerful revelation that God—I AM—was with them. This is the same God whose message Isaiah proclaimed:

> But now, O Israel, the LORD who created you says: "Do not be afraid, for I have ransomed you. I have called you by name; you are mine. When you go through deep waters and great trouble, I will be with you. When you go through rivers of difficulty, you will not drown! When you walk through the fire of oppression, you will not be burned up; the flames will not consume you. For I am the LORD, your God, the Holy One of Israel, your Savior...you are precious to me. You are honored, and I love you. Do not be afraid, for I am with you" (Isaiah 43:1-5).

"I am here"—three simple words packed with promise and spoken to replace fear with courage. They reminded the disciples that they were not alone in the storm. Almighty God, the eternal One, Creator and sustainer of life, protector and Savior, was with them.

Imagine the scene! The wind continued to blow. The waves continued to splash and soak and slosh. But into the storm walked the great I AM. His disciples felt terrorized and traumatized, but Almighty God met His loved ones at their point of need and calmed their fears.

I AM, the all-wise, all-powerful God, is the same yesterday, today, and forever. He still meets His followers in the midst of their storms. I'll always remember sailing in gale force winds that day, and I'll forever cherish His words: *Don't be afraid. Be still and know that I am God.* They calmed my fears then, and they calm my fears each time a personal storm blows into my life.

Look back to Isaiah 43:1-5 for a moment. When a storm strikes, I run to these verses and find consolation in the truths they teach about the character of the great I AM.

- Because I AM created me, He knows everything about me—past, present, and future. He understands what frightens me and how to soothe my anxious thoughts.

- Because He paid my ransom with the life blood of His Son, I know He loves me more than words can say. The depth of His love warrants my trust, even when bad things happen.

- Because He knows my name and claims me as His own, I know He treasures me.

- Because He promises to be with me when I go through deep waters and great trouble, I know I'm not alone in the storms. I find peace in His presence.

- Because He promises that I won't drown in the rivers of

difficulty, I have confidence in His ability to sustain me regardless of what comes my way.

• Because He promises that the fire of oppression won't consume me, I can face hardships with courage.

• Because He identifies Himself as my God and Savior, I know He's personally interested in my life. He hasn't abandoned me to navigate life on my own. He takes responsibility for me as His child.

• Because He considers me as precious, honored, and loved, I know He holds me close to His heart. Again, the depth of His love for me deserves my full-blown trust.

• Because He promises to be with me, I am assured of His constant presence. And because He's always with me, I need not be afraid.

If Bruce Larson is correct, we'll never live without fear. Personal storms will strike when we least expect, and fear will rear its head. But in the midst of our scary situations, fear need not paralyze or consume us. Rather, we can move beyond its clutches as we appropriate for our lives Jesus' reassuring and oft-spoken command, "Fear not."

Perhaps a huge storm has engulfed you. Fear has become your constant companion—one with whom you'd rather part company. Don't despair! You can move beyond it by immersing yourself in the Word of God, believing its promises, and clinging to what you know to be true about God.

Wanda, a woman I met at a recent women's retreat, has done this. When she told me her story, I knew instantly that it belonged in this book.

Wanda's Story

Wanda's countenance glowed, and her smile lit up the room where several women had gathered to pray before the retreat officially began.

One by one, the women poured out their hearts to God, asking Him to visit the weekend in a deep and meaningful way. When Wanda's turn came, she spoke with Him as to an intimate friend. The ease and familiarity with which she prayed told me that she'd spent much time in private conversation with Him. The next day, as she shared her past with me, I knew my hunch was correct.

Wanda was 19 years old and a new believer when she married her 20-year-old boyfriend. He was using cocaine, but she figured that wasn't a cause for major concern. After all, she'd used drugs too, but her life had turned around. She thought he would come clean and follow Jesus with her. She assumed they'd live happily ever after, raising their two children and enjoying the security of a loving family. She was wrong.

Rather than enjoying a stable and happy marriage, Wanda spent the next 20 years visiting her husband in prison, attending meetings with lawyers and parole officers and counselors, and spending time in treatment centers. Her heart ached as her husband's behavior broke their children's trust in him.

During those dark decades, Wanda responded by immersing herself in God's Word on a regular basis. There she found encouragement and fresh reminders of His love for her. She discovered Him to be her husband, provider, strength, and support. The Bible's promises spoke life to her, and she experienced comfort and refuge in God's presence.

Besides drawing strength from God's Word, Wanda prayed. And prayed. And prayed. Finally, it seemed as though her pleas had been heard. Her husband overcame his addiction and attended Bible college for two years. He regained his children's trust. The couple bought their first house and invested in a business.

The sky was blue and the weather balmy for two years, but then the black clouds rolled back in, and the storm broke loose again. Wanda's husband returned to his cocaine addiction. The couple lost their home and their business. Their marriage crumbled, and Wanda became a single mom with two teenagers. Looking for a fresh start, she moved to a city where she knew only her sister. One year and five months later the storm erupted with a fury beyond her wildest imagination.

Wanda's phone rang at 2:30 a.m. on March 17, 2001. It stopped ringing before she reached it, but the call display revealed her son's cell phone. He was at a friend's birthday party and had planned to spend the night there.

That's strange, thought Wanda. *Why would Travis phone me at this hour?* She returned the call, and one of Travis' friends answered.

"Something terrible has happened!" said the boy. "Travis has been shot! It's very, very serious. He's on his way to the hospital!"

Wanda was directed to the emergency room when she arrived at the hospital. There lay her 19-year-old son, motionless. His shirt had been ripped off. Dried blood caked his face. A small hole pierced his face beside his right eye, and his eye was swollen shut.

Some folks would curse God in such a moment. Others might descend into dumbfounded shock. Some might be overwhelmed with fear and what-ifs. *What if he dies? What if he has brain damage? What if he never awakens from the coma?*

The previous two years' losses and adjustments had left Wanda feeling as though she'd been kicked in the gut. She'd barely caught her breath. Now this.

Lord, how could this be happening? He's so innocent. He doesn't lead a lifestyle that invites this kind of crisis. She touched her son's face and held his hand. And as she did, she sensed God's comforting voice: *I am with you. Look not at the circumstances. Look only to Me. My grace will be sufficient for you moment by moment.*

A sweet sense of God's presence enveloped Wanda. His Word filled her thoughts and touched her at her deepest point of need in a most amazing, specific way: "If your heart is broken, you'll find GOD right there; if you're kicked in the gut, he'll help you catch your breath" (Psalm 34:18 MSG).

Another Scripture came to mind. She clung to this one over the next five days while she sat beside Travis' bedside and watched the life-support machine breathe for him. "Give your entire attention to what God is doing right now, and don't get worked up about what may or may not happen tomorrow. God will help you deal with whatever hard things come up when the time comes" (Matthew 6:34 MSG).

Wanda purposed to believe God's promise to help her deal with the hard thing at hand. She focused on His faithfulness, His comfort, and His strength, and she refused to panic over possible what-ifs. She held Travis' hand, lifted her heart in songs of worship to the Lord, and refused to be overcome by fear for her son's life. By doing so, she found His grace to be sufficient one moment at a time.

"Some people couldn't understand why I wasn't crying and tied in emotional knots," says Wanda. "They thought I didn't care deeply about my son. But that wasn't the case. I could deal with the storm because I knew that the God I love and serve was bigger than it, and that He's able to work all things together for the good of those who love Him."[3]

When Wanda finished telling me her story, I understood the reason behind her peaceful countenance and powerful prayers. Her walk with God and her understanding of His character had kept her steadfast through the storm and through the following weeks as Travis recovered.

The same can be true for you and me. Life changes in a blink. Scary situations happen. What will keep us from falling into its grip? Only our relationship with God and our subsequent understanding of who He is. That alone will be the anchor that holds us firm and enables us to move beyond fear. But there's a catch—the strength to move beyond fear comes only with time and effort.

Prepare for the Storm

Living on Canada's west coast, we experience several winter storms each year. Sometimes they're fierce enough to knock over trees, cause power outages, and delay the ferries. They're inconvenient.

They add hassle to everyday life. But they're nothing in comparison to the hurricanes that ravage other parts of North America.

Occasionally we hear news reports of approaching hurricanes in states such as Florida or Louisiana. We watch video clips of people in those locations preparing for the onslaught. They cover glass windows with plywood. They stash extra supplies of bottled water and groceries. They anchor loose items in their yards or store them away. Sometimes, depending on the forecast, they run for cover in another city. The point is, they know the storm is coming, and they prepare for it. Heaven help the soul who knows a hurricane is approaching but flaunts a careless attitude.

Life in the physical realm carries countless analogies to the spiritual realm. Unlike many storms, however, scary stuff usually threatens havoc without warning. This could be a depressing thought—enough to taint our mornings with dread about potential disasters or turn us into incurable pessimists, searching the skies for nasty black clouds. I don't mean to ruin your day! Au contraire!

Life's storms often show up unannounced. We don't know the day or the hour they'll arrive, but that makes no difference if we've prepared. We can stand firm in foul weather, confident in the presence of the mighty God, I AM. We can keep our eyes on the Savior rather than the wind and waves that threaten to topple us. We can rest in our heavenly Father's loving care as Wanda did, knowing that He's bigger than any storm that comes our way. But preparation requires effort, just as homeowners exert effort to prepare their homes for a hurricane.

So how do we prepare? By protecting our minds. By filling them with words of life and truth.

According to author John Ortberg, we are what we think. "The way you think creates your attitudes; the way you think shapes your emotions; the way you think governs your behavior; the way you think deeply influences your immune system and vulnerability to illness. Everything about you flows out of the way you think."[4]

This reminds me of the old adage, "We are what we eat." A steady diet of potato chips, ice cream, and chocolate cake yields a few unwanted pounds and extra padding. "Over the lips and onto the hips," as someone once said. Our bodies and brains will pay the price if we consistently stuff our stomachs with junk food. On the other hand, a menu that includes lots of water, fresh fruits, raw veggies, and whole grains will help keep our bodies healthy and fit. Simple.

So it is with our minds. We are what we think. Exposing our minds to material that promotes promiscuity or infidelity as the norm damages us. Filling them with junk food like gruesome movies or warped song lyrics injures us. Stuffing them with gossip about the neighbors or criticism of the pastor hurts us. The junk food we relish feeds us empty calories and gives us no substance from which to draw strength for the battle. The storm dumps, and we're devastated.

But feeding our minds with words of life and truth makes us strong and vibrant. Those words equip us for the struggle by reminding us who's in charge. They give us hope by showing us that God sees the big picture, from beginning to end, and He has purposes that are much higher than our loftiest imaginings. They reveal God's character and enable us to keep our thoughts on Him when we feel as though we've been thrust overboard without a life jacket.

"Whether we are filled with confidence or fear depends on the kind of thoughts that habitually occupy our minds," says Ortberg.[5] That makes sense, doesn't it? If we want to stand against the storm, we need to prepare by occupying our minds with thoughts of God's awesome power and strength, His love for His children, His ability to do the impossible, His compassion for those who hurt, and His wisdom that exceeds our understanding. We need to familiarize ourselves with biblical accounts that show what He's done in the past and reveal His promises for the present and future. And we must recall His faithful and mighty acts we've already witnessed or experienced.

Doing these things guarantees a prepared heart when the storm hits. Wanda's story verifies this. For two decades she'd soaked in the Word of God and developed a close friendship with its Author. When the phone call came, she experienced the fulfillment of the promise in Isaiah 26:3: "You will keep in perfect peace all who trust in you, whose thoughts are fixed on you!"

Jan Turner's story also proves this is true. Facing life as a quadruple amputee seemed insurmountable at times, but filling her mind with truth gave her the needed strength to press forward. She recalls reading Psalm 103:2,4: "Praise the LORD, I tell myself, and never forget the good things he does for me...He ransoms me from death and surrounds me with love and tender mercies." Then she made her choice.

I will do what the Word says. I will praise the Lord. I will recognize the benefits that are mine because He has ransomed me from death and surrounds me with love.

Another truth that buoyed Jan in the midst of battering waves was 2 Corinthians 4:17-18:

> For our present troubles are quite small and won't last very long. Yet they produce for us an immeasurably great glory that will last forever! So we don't look at the troubles we can see right now; rather, we look forward to what we have not yet seen. For the troubles we see will soon be over, but the joys to come will last forever.

I will not get caught up in this natural realm, Jan thought. *I'm living on this earth, and I'm facing an uncertain future, but it's temporal. No matter what happens, heaven is my real home.*

Truth filled Jan with peace and gave her hope. Wherever she tells her story, she leaves her audiences with wise advice: "Gaze at the promises; glance at the problems. Remember, God is faithful. He'll always see us through."

Are you prepared for the storm, my dear reader? Are you filling your mind with truth? Are you focusing your thoughts where they belong day by day so that you'll be equipped to stand steadfast when

FOCUS ON GOD,
NOT ON FEAR

How can we train our minds to focus on God? Here are eight practical tips you may find helpful:

1. Write Scripture promises on three-by-five cards. Post them where you'll see them often. I post cards on the wall near the kitchen sink and near my computer monitor.

2. Memorize and meditate on Scripture. Mull over a particular verse as you go about your daily activities or as you fall asleep at night. It will become automatic ammo when fearful thoughts pop into your mind.

3. Fill your home with praise and worship music. If you're a contemporary music fan as I am, expand your horizons and buy a CD of the good ol' hymns. Many were penned in the midst of incredible heartache. You'll find some lyrics that reflect an intimate understanding of God's character.

4. Seek silence in God's presence. Find a time that works for you and steal away for a few minutes several times each week. No prayer requests allowed! Just praise-filled thoughts and reflections on His faithfulness.

5. Make an altar of remembrance to celebrate God's faithfulness. Collect ornaments as little visual aids to remind you of specific events in which God protected you, provided for you, or answered a specific prayer. Place the visual aids on a decorative shelf.

6. Take problems to the Lord rather than to a friend. Phoning a friend and seeking her advice before praying is easy and sometimes automatic. Reverse the order and seek God's counsel first.

7. Talk to the Lord throughout your day. Recognize His presence in all your activities, including the mundane.

8. Read material that directs your thoughts toward God. Toss the supermarket tabloids and sleazy romance novels. Subscribe to a Christian women's magazine. Check out good fiction and nonfiction books from the church library.

the ugly weather rolls in? If so, I'm thrilled for you. If not, I fear for you. I pray you'll understand the importance of being prepared and choose to take action.

Seeing God in the Storm

Remember Job? This guy was prepared. He was also the richest man around. Besides that, he was a man of complete integrity, blameless in business dealings and passionate about his kids' purity.

One minute Job's horizon looked sunny and cloud free. A nanosecond later, a personal tsunami broadsided him when a messenger arrived, breathless and bearing bad news. Then a second messenger ran in, and a third. They told Job that his livestock and servants had been wiped out—either stolen, burned by fire, or murdered by marauders. His wealth was suddenly a mere memory. Before the third messenger finished speaking, number four arrived with news that carried the potential to destroy anyone with lesser faith.

Job's seven sons and three daughters had been dining at the oldest brother's house when a powerful wind swept in from the desert. Its force knocked the walls down and crushed them (Job 1:13-19). Imagine! Losing one child is unthinkable, but ten? Who could survive a storm of such magnitude?

Job.

He stood up and tore his robe in grief. Then he shaved his head and fell to the ground before God crying, "I came naked from my mother's womb, and I will be stripped of everything when I die. The LORD gave me everything I had, and the LORD has taken it away. Praise the name of the LORD!" (Job 1:21).

How could Job respond like this when the tsunami struck? By focusing on the Lord, not on his circumstances. If he had given his attention solely to his situation, I guarantee his tongue would have uttered anything but praise.

Poor Job—the storm continued its assault. The next blow came when oozing, painful boils broke out on his body and covered him from head to foot. There sat our hero, in an ash heap, scraping himself with a chunk of broken pottery. His wife stared at him in disgust and offered a piece of not-so-helpful advice: "Are you still trying to maintain your integrity? Curse God and die" (Job 2:9). Again, Job's response reflected his God-centered focus. "Should we accept only good things from the hand of God and never anything bad?" (Job 2:10).

Time rolled on. Three so-called friends knocked on Job's door and proceeded to pepper him with home-brewed theology about the reasons for his suffering. That's when Job's faith began to teeter and he admitted losing the sense of God's presence. "I go east, but he is not there. I go west, but I cannot find him. I do not see him in the north, for he is hidden. I turn to the south, but I cannot find him." The winds of doubt howled and harassed him, but Job refused to give up hope. Once again he expressed an affirmation of trust. "But he knows where I am going. And when he has tested me like gold in a fire, he will pronounce me innocent" (Job 23:8-10).

Can you identify with Job's emotions? Have you ever felt as though God has abandoned you to fight the wind and waves alone? If so, don't despair! Cling to His promises. He has stated, "I will never fail you. I will never forsake you" (Hebrews 13:5). Even in the darkest hour, when fear threatens to swamp your little boat, know that God is with you. Sometimes embracing that knowledge requires a sheer act of the will.

Jerry Bridges says that "trust is not a passive state of mind. It is a vigorous act of the soul by which we choose to lay hold of the promises of God and cling to them despite the fear that at times seeks to overwhelm us." [6] Sometimes bad things happen. Personal, tragic tsunamis catch you off guard. You might not understand God's ways, and you might lose a sense of His presence.

Regardless of your feelings, lay hold of His truth. Ask God for faith to fit the need. Hang on with all your might the same way Job did, sister. If you do, you'll see and experience God in ways that will leave you standing in awe. Job emerged from the storm with words that prove this is possible. "I had heard about you before, but now I have seen you with my own eyes. I take back everything I said, and I sit in dust and ashes to show my repentance" (Job 42:5-6).

I had heard about you before, but now I have seen you with my own eyes. These words deserve more than a second glance. They tell us we can settle for an academic knowledge of who God is rather than an active life-changing understanding of His character. You know how it goes—the pastor's words enter our ears and get stuck in our brains rather than absorbed into our hearts. And there we sit, entrenched in our spiritual rut until...*whoosh!* A tsunami sweeps in and rearranges our lives.

What's left when the storm subsides? If we've sought God and His Word in our distress, we'll emerge with a heart understanding of who He is. Hardships become opportunities to experience the sermons we've heard about His strength and power, His mercy and love, and His provision and wisdom.

Job's encounter with God left him humbled, sitting in dust and ashes and repentant for arguing with I AM about his circumstances. He recognized his own finite and foolish humanity in comparison to God's bigness, and he turned his attitude around.

As for you and me, I doubt that a fresh glimpse of God's character will compel us to plunk ourselves onto a heap of ashes hauled from the woodstove and dumped onto the front lawn. But even the slightest peek of who God is should drive us to our knees and lift our hearts in praise.

I want to close this chapter with one of my favorite hymns. It was written by Lina Sandell Berg, a young woman born in Sweden in 1832. She was the daughter of a parish minister, a frail youngster who spent hours sitting in her father's study rather than playing outside with her peers.

When Lina was 26 years old, she accompanied her father on a trip. But tragedy struck before they reached their destination. The ship lurched, throwing her father overboard. He drowned as Lina watched helplessly from the ship's deck.[7]

Lina's lyrics reveal a life that has seen God in the storm. Her response to the personal tsunami has blessed countless lives around the world. I pray that it will bless yours with peace.

DAY BY DAY

Lina Sandell Berg

Day by day and with each passing moment,
Strength I find to meet my trials here;
Trusting in my Father's wise bestowment,
I've no cause for worry or for fear.
He whose heart is kind beyond all measure
Gives unto each day what He deems best.
Lovingly, its part of pain and pleasure,
Mingling toil with peace and rest.

Every day the Lord Himself is near me
With a special mercy for each hour;
All my cares He fain would bear, and cheer me,
He whose name is Counselor and Power.
The protection of His child and treasure
Is a charge that on Himself He laid;
"As thy days, thy strength shall be in measure,"
This the pledge to me He made.

Help me then in every tribulation
So to trust Thy promises, O Lord,
That I lose not faith's sweet consolation
Offered me within Thy holy Word.
Help me, Lord, when toil and trouble meeting,
E'er to take, as from a father's hand,
One by one, the days, the moments fleeting,
Till I reach the promised land.

✦ POINTS FOR PROGRESS ✦

Max Lucado wrote the following thoughts about Job:

> All his life, Job had been a good man. All his life, he had believed in God. All his life, he had discussed God, had notions about him, and had prayed to him.
>
> *But in the storm Job sees him!...*
>
> Something tells me that Job would do it all again, if that's what it took to hear God's voice and stand in the Presence. Even if God left him with his bedsores and bills, Job would do it again.
>
> For God gave Job more than Job ever dreamed. God gave Job Himself.[8]

1. Describe one or two storms you've experienced.

2. Job's personal tsunami revealed God's character to him in a new way. What character qualities of God have you discovered through your storms?

3. How has that knowledge impacted your outlook and your ability to handle subsequent difficulties?

4. Scripture says that God is able to use even negative events for His glory and the good of those who love Him. How have you seen this principle fulfilled in your own life?

5. List five practical things you can do to encourage another woman who is in the midst of a storm.

✦ PROMISES TO PONDER ✦

Because the Sovereign LORD helps me, I will not be dismayed. Therefore, I have set my face like a stone, determined to do his will. And I know that I will triumph...Who among you fears the LORD and obeys

his servant? If you are walking in darkness, without a
ray of light, trust in the LORD and rely on your God
(Isaiah 50:7,10).

The ropes of death surrounded me;
   the floods of destruction swept over me.
The grave wrapped its ropes around me;
   death itself stared me in the face.
But in my distress I cried out to the LORD;
   yes, I prayed to my God for help.
He heard me from his sanctuary;
   my cry reached his ears...
As for God, his way is perfect.
   All the LORD's promises prove true.
   He is a shield to all who look to him for protection
(Psalm 18:4-6,30).

O LORD, how long will you forget me? Forever?
   How long will you look the other way?
How long must I struggle with anguish in my soul,
   with sorrow in my heart every day?...
But I trust in your unfailing love.
   I will rejoice because you have rescued me.
I will sing to the LORD because he has been so good
   to me (Psalm 13:1-2,5-6).

✦ PRAYING THE PROMISES ✦

*Father, I praise You because You are sovereign. I'm grateful
that You, the blessed controller of all things, are my helper.
I have every reason to be confident and not be dismayed. I
will do whatever You ask, and I know that I will triumph.
When the storm rages and all appears black around me, I
will trust and rely on You. Amen.*

God, sometimes I feel as though I can't go on. I'm crying to You in my distress. Hear me from Your sanctuary. I know Your way is perfect. All Your promises are true. You are my shield, and I trust You to protect me. Amen.

Father, I feel as though You're looking the other way and have forgotten about me. My heart is filled with sorrow. How long must it stay that way? But in the midst of my storm, I will trust in Your love. You have rescued me from my troubles. I praise Your name for being good to me...all the time. Amen.

What *will* Tomorrow Bring?

Fear makes the wolf bigger than he is.

GERMAN PROVERB

Today's headlines give us reason to ask, what will tomorrow bring? They reveal concerns of international proportion—AIDS, terrorism, war, global warming, mad cow disease, drought, hurricanes, tsunamis, and earthquakes. Yikes! When I opened my e-mail recently, an online newspaper asked, "Will the church be ready *when,* not *if,* the bird flu pandemic strikes?"

Some people read such headlines and brush them off: *I can't control these things, so why worry about them?* They choose to believe that ignorance is bliss. Other folks stew and fret, numbing their fear with alcohol or drugs, or seeking consolation from fortune-tellers. Some pursue freedom-from-fear-forever cures such as listening to recorded subliminal messages while they sleep. And then there are those who build underground bunkers and stock them with weapons, canned food, and bottled water, just in case. If possible, some people would love to simply find a secret hiding place and avoid the chaos.

The majority of us, however, struggle with fears that never make the headlines. We stay awake at night worrying about what tomorrow will bring if the lump we feel in our breast turns out to be cancer. We lose sleep wondering about what might happen if our house doesn't sell for the asking price, or worrying about what will happen to our daughter if she marries the dud she's dating.

Every woman alive asks the same question at one time or another: *What will tomorrow bring?* We might not express it in those exact words, but the essence remains the same. Circumstances change, plans fail, dreams shatter, and suddenly the future as we've envisioned it assumes an entirely different face. Fear is often an automatic response. I faced this recently.

Fear Hits Home

There I was, hunched over my computer keyboard and writing this chapter. That's when the phone rang. (Sheesh—why does the phone so often bear bad news?) It was my mother, who lives nearly a thousand miles away. "I have some sad news about your dad," she said.

One year ago, doctors diagnosed Dad with prostate cancer and placed him on hormone treatments. Blood tests proved that the treatments were working, and his health seemed stable. But Mom's call told me that circumstances had changed. The hormone treatments were no longer effective.

My mind instantly descended into a pit of what-ifs: *What if Dad starts experiencing a lot of pain? What if he passes away quickly? What if he dies slowly? What if Mom can't handle watching her husband of 53 years go through this?* Fear gripped me. I found myself staring into the unknown and wondering what tomorrow might look like for my parents.

Thankfully, I recognized what was happening and was able to turn my focus around. But that hasn't always been the case. When I conducted the survey about fear, most participants admitted that they too wrestle with the fear of the unknown.

Several gals said they have children with special needs. They fear a future that requires caring for sons and daughters who will likely remain dependent for life.

Others, whose marriages are barely surviving, say they fear a future that may involve divorce. They'd envisioned growing old with their spouse, traveling together, and sharing laughs at their grand-kids' antics. But the road ahead now looms lonely and dark.

Several said they'd married young and had entertained fanta-sies of living happily ever after. Years later, crippling diseases have ravaged their husbands' bodies. Employment is impossible, playing with the kids is a strain, and communication between spouses is a thing of the past. Only heaven knows what the future holds.

Numerous women indicated fear for their children's future, especially for those who are involved with drugs, alcohol, and pro-miscuous lifestyles. Will their kids realize their dead-end path and change their ways, or will they continue their behavior and reap a heap of sad or tragic consequences? What will their tomorrows bring if they don't turn around?

All of us, at some point, peer down the road that stretches before us and wonder what detours and potholes we'll encounter before we reach our final destination. Deep down in our hearts, if we're fol-lowers of Jesus Christ, we rest assured that heaven awaits. Starvation and sickness, war and poverty, death and pain—all the major scary stuff—will no longer exist.

That sounds great, and we look forward to that day, but we're not there yet. The road ahead no doubt contains troubles we must traverse enroute to the pearly gates. Like it or not, we're going to have to navigate a few. So how can we become like the woman who wraps herself with strength and dignity and who laughs with no fear of the future (Proverbs 31:25)?

In light of today's global and personal uncertainties, how could anyone live with such a confident attitude? Believe it or not, it *is* pos-sible. Meet Jennifer Rothschild, follower of God and an international women's ministry leader. She knows what it means to smile at an uncertain future. And her response deserves our close attention.

Jennifer's Journey

Jennifer will never forget the day doctors delivered her grim diagnosis. She was only 15 years old when the doctors told her, "You have an eye disease called retinitis pigmentosa. There is no cure and no way to repair the damage already done. Your retinas will deteriorate until you are blind...totally blind."

Silence shrouded the family car on the trip home from the eye institute. Jennifer's parents sat in the front seat, stunned by the doctor's words. The teen sat behind them, wrestling with shock and grief. Questions swirled through her mind: *How will I finish high school? How will I know what I look like? Will boys want to date me? Will I ever marry?*

In a few brief moments, Jennifer's bright and promising future was stripped of all semblance of security. The doctors' words left her peering into the unknown and wondering, *What will tomorrow bring?*

When at last she and her folks arrived at home, she wandered into the living room and sat down at the piano. Jennifer had never played by ear before, but that afternoon a familiar melody flowed from her fingers and filled the room as she reflected on these words:

> When peace, like a river, attendeth my way,
> When sorrows like sea billows roll,
> Whatever my lot, Thou has taught me to say,
> It is well, it is well with my soul.
>
> Tho Satan should buffet, tho trials should come,
> Let this blest assurance control,
> That Christ hath regarded my helpless estate
> And shed His own blood for my soul.
>
> And, Lord, haste the day when my faith shall be sight,
> The clouds be rolled back as a scroll;
> The trump shall resound and the Lord shall descend,
> Even so—it is well with my soul.

The hymn "It Is Well with My Soul" had been penned in 1873 by Horatio Spafford after the drowning deaths of his four daughters. The grieving father recognized that even though he couldn't understand God's ways at the present time, he would someday see clearly. That knowledge brought peace in the midst of deep sorrow and unanswerable questions.

Jennifer felt the same way.

"I think God guided my heart and hands to play that hymn," Jennifer told me as we chatted by phone. "Some people say it was a miracle that I could sit down at the piano that day and begin to play by ear for the first time. Perhaps it was. Who knows? But to me, there was a bigger miracle that dark day of shock, loss, and quiet sorrow. The real miracle was not that I played 'It Is Well with My Soul,' but that it actually *was* well with my soul."

"In light of facing an unknown future, how could you respond in such a way?" I asked. Her answer inspired me then, and it challenges me to this day.

"God had so captured me as a nine-year-old that I couldn't be angry," said Jennifer. "He'd demonstrated His love to me through the gift of His Son, and I'd sensed His presence in my life. I just couldn't be mad at Him."[1]

When my future looks uncertain and I worry about tomorrow, I recall Jennifer's words. If she can say it is well with her soul, so can you and I. That ability doesn't stem from a power generated from within ourselves, but solely from understanding that God loves us and walks with us moment by moment.

When the doctors told Jennifer her diagnosis, she clung to that truth. It didn't guarantee an absence of fear, but it gave her the strength and courage necessary to move forward, trusting God to walk with her and to fulfill His plan for her life. Her attitude revealed what she believed to be true about God.

It's an age-old scenario. Men and women throughout history have faced frightening futures, and their responses have revealed their understanding of who God is. Those who believe that His presence goes with them demonstrate courage and peace. And they're the blessed ones who enter the promised land, the place where God reveals Himself in new and exciting ways.

Two Perspectives

One hot afternoon, a dozen men stood at the border of a foreign nation, preparing to perform a secret mission—to spy out the promised land (Numbers 13:1–14:11). "I want to know all the details," said their boss, Moses. "Do the cities have walls, or are they unprotected? Is the soil fertile or poor? Are the people strong or weak? Are they few or many? Are there many trees? Tell me everything we need to know so we can plan our attack accordingly."

The 12 men bid Moses goodbye and trekked through the land for 40 days. When they returned, their report revealed two outlooks as opposite as black is from white. Ten spies agreed that the promised land looked even better than promising. It looked *magnificent.* And to prove it, they had grapes unlike anything we'd find in the local grocery store. But despite the good stuff, they focused on the negatives:

> We arrived in the land you sent us to see, and it is indeed a magnificent country—a land flowing with milk and honey. Here is some of its fruit as proof. But the people living there are powerful, and their cities and towns are fortified and very large. We also saw the descendants of Anak who are living there!…We can't go up against them! They are stronger than we are!…The land we explored will swallow up any who go to live there. All the people we saw were huge. We even saw giants there, the descendants of Anak. We felt like grasshoppers next to them, and that's what we looked like to them! (Numbers 13:29-33).

Granted, the descendants of Anak *were* intimidating. They made Goliath look like a peewee, and that frightened the ten. "The odds against us are too great," they might have said. "We're as good as dead. Those guys will squash us like bugs!"

Was this a skewed perspective or what? They focused on the scary stuff rather than on God's promise to be with them. Fear paralyzed them, and they refused to enter the hard places into which God was calling them even though He'd already promised victory.

Enter Caleb with perspective number two. He refuted the other spies' objections with a simple and straightforward response: "Let's go at once to take the land...We can certainly conquer it!" (Numbers 13:30). You'd think his enthusiasm might have changed the other guys' minds, but that wasn't the case. They wailed and whined and stirred up their audience who, in turn, began to weep and complain against Moses and Aaron.

Caleb tried again. This time Joshua joined him:

> The land we explored is a wonderful land! And if the LORD is pleased with us, he will bring us safely into that land and give it to us. It is a rich land flowing with milk and honey, and he will give it to us! Do not rebel against the LORD, and don't be afraid of the people of the land. They are only helpless prey to us! They have no protection, but the LORD is with us! Don't be afraid of them! (Numbers 14:7-9).

From where did these two bold believers get their positive perspective? Certainly not from their own strength or trumped-up self-confidence. It flowed from understanding truth—the Lord's presence was with them. If He was pleased with them, He would bring them into that land. His presence was their protection.

Why did only two of the 12 spies feel this way? Theirs was the minority report because placing faith in an unseen God goes against human nature. Talking about trusting God in the face of the unknown is easy, but we often lose faith when the crunch comes. Like the ten spies, we jettison the truth and settle for what's comfortable rather than what's best or what might stretch us.

Why is that so often the case? We give up because we lack a proper understanding of God. His Word describes Him as an all-powerful, all-present Creator, but when we face a frightening future as the spies did, our mind's eye sees Him dwindle to munchkin size.

> I strongly believe that the way we live is a consequence of the size of our God. The problem many of us have is that our God is too small. We are not convinced that we are absolutely safe in the hands of a fully competent, all-knowing, ever-present God. When we wake up in the morning, what happens if we live with a small God? We live in a constant state of fear and anxiety because every-thing depends on us. Our mood will be governed by our circumstances. We will live in a universe that leaves us deeply vulnerable.[2]

How big is your God? Big enough to form the seas and hold the waters in the palm of His hand? Big enough to throw the stars into space and control the constellations? Big enough to weigh the earth's dust in a scale? I hope you're nodding yes!

This, ladies, is the God who promises His presence. If we're His children through a personal relationship with Jesus Christ, He will never leave us. How then can we be afraid?

Take a quiet moment before reading further. Ask the Lord to examine your heart. If your attitude resembles that of the ten spies, ask Him to forgive you for doubting His greatness and for allowing circumstances to govern your mood. Ask Him to correct your understanding of who He is and to give you the power to apply that knowledge to whatever fears you struggle with. Thank Him in advance for what He's going to do in your life as you choose to believe He is who He says He is.

The Promised Land and God's Purposes

Fear. The devil's modus operandi is to manipulate you with the mysterious, to taunt you with the unknown. Fear of death, fear of failure, fear of God, fear of tomorrow—

his arsenal is vast. His goal? To create cowardly, joyless souls. He doesn't want you to make the journey to the mountain. He figures if he can rattle you enough, you will take your eyes off the peaks and settle for a dull existence in the flatlands.[3]

How true! The devil loves it when we settle for mediocrity. And fear is one of his favorite tactics to accomplish his purposes. Few are the faithful who truly enter the promised land and experience God as He desires to reveal Himself to His followers. Like the ten spies, too many believers succumb to fear and settle for life on the flatlands. They focus on the challenges ahead and refuse to budge, saying, "Nope—I'm not going there!" The result? They never enter the promised land and witness God work in extraordinary ways. What a shame.

Jennifer's life is a great example of a Joshua-Caleb attitude. She refused to settle for a dull existence in the flatlands. As a result, her journey has been filled with opportunities to trust God in the face of the unknown, and she has discovered His blessings for obedience. For instance, eager for independence at age 18, she applied to attend a Christian liberal arts college 90 miles from home. Fear gripped her the day before her departure.

"I can't do this! What was I thinking?" Jennifer cried to her mom. She recited reasons she couldn't go. "I don't know anyone there! Who will tell me what food is on my plate? Who will tell me if my clothes are clean?"

Her mother wiped her own tears and told Jennifer that she must follow through on her plans, but that she could return home after two weeks if the experience proved too difficult.

Before the trial period ended, Jennifer met sophomore student Philip Rothschild. "If it's possible for a blind woman to experience love at first sight, I did!" Jennifer says, laughing.

My crisis of leaving home for college typifies life. When we're standing on the brink of uncertainty, it's natural to feel fear. Sometimes that fear stops us from stepping into the hard places where God is calling us, but unless we're willing to trade our fear for fight, we may forfeit His greatest blessings. Obviously for me, that greatest blessing was my husband. I would have forfeited that if my mother hadn't coaxed me to be courageous.

The past 20 years have dealt Jennifer other frightening situations due to her blindness, but she has refused to let them stop her from climbing the mountain. Rather, she has chosen to face her fear and has come to consider her blindness as a gift.

"God has used the blindness to remind me in a tangible way that I'm fully dependent on Him," she says. "I can embrace it realizing that God's using it to keep me close to Him and to help me connect with Him more intimately."

One of the blessings I enjoy as a writer and speaker is meeting other Christian women. Many talk about their desire to pursue God's purpose for their lives, but time and time again, they tell me that fear is keeping them in the flatlands. Once in a while, however, a woman will tell me that God has placed a dream within her heart and that she's actively doing something about it.

Theresa, a mother of three young children and a former spa owner, is one of those women. She approached me at the end of a weekend retreat and told me her story. She'd trained as a massage therapist and had found great fulfillment in serving seniors in the local continuing care facility. A year prior to the retreat, however, she began sensing that God wanted to expand her ministry. She started formulating a plan. Bit by bit, it unfolded into something beyond her wildest imagination.

"I just don't know if I can do this," Theresa said.

"What makes you feel that way?" I asked.

"Fear," she admitted. "What if I fail? What if things don't happen as I envision them?"

"If God is calling you to do this, the details are His responsibility,"

I said. Then I gave her a tidbit that someone else had given me when I was dipping my toes into the publishing industry waters. "That doesn't mean it will be a quick and easy journey, but if God is in this, keep going until He tells you to stop."

Nearly four months passed before we spoke again. When I asked her how her plan was progressing, she said, "The powers that be are still analyzing my proposal. At this point it's just a waiting game, but I'm learning a lot in the process."

"How's the fear factor these days?" I asked.

"Well, fear still creeps in," she admitted. "I think Satan wants me to second-guess the vision God's given me. But I keep turning to God and saying, 'This is Your work. Do with it whatever You want.' "

Curious, I asked Theresa if she'd found a particular Scripture helpful as she wrestled with her fear. She thought for a moment and then answered, "Yes. I hear one verse a lot in my head: 'I will never leave you nor forsake you' " (Joshua 1:5 NIV). She paused for another moment and then added, "I hear those words whenever I'm feeling overwhelmed or discouraged or afraid. I'm coming to realize that even when I don't feel God near, He is there. I cling to that verse!"[4]

Theresa is heading out of the flatlands and toward the peaks! Fear of the unknown confronts her frequently, but she's choosing to focus on truth instead. And the truth is, God has promised His presence in her life.

This is what Katie Brazelton, founder of Pathway to Purpose Ministry, says:

> Did you know that God does not need our courage to proceed with his plans? We can pick any one of a number of Bible stories—Jonah, Moses, Esther, or Peter, for example—and see that God accomplished his work in the midst of someone's fear. So, we really have only two choices when it comes to fears related to fulfilling our life

purpose. The first is to complete God's assignments while kicking and screaming in fear. And our second choice is to make the entire journey easier by beginning today to give our fears to God, or at least to trust that he is with us as we do his work.[5]

Amen to that! Courage comes when we act upon the truth of God's promise to be with us. That doesn't mean our fears will suddenly sprout wings and fly away, but it means we'll have the freedom to move forward despite feeling afraid. I can testify to that.

For 20 years I'd dreamed about becoming a writer, but real life kept me too preoccupied to pursue it. Besides, dreaming was safe—it didn't force me into unfamiliar territory. But when the opportunity to proceed finally presented itself and God appeared to be leading in that direction, I was faced with a decision: remain in the flatlands or begin my ascent up the mountaintop. I chose to climb, but that decision came with a bundle of fear attached.

The day before I left home to attend my first writers' conference, I sat with my husband at our kitchen table and cried because the unknown loomed before me like a black hole waiting to suck me in. I would be leaving the next morning to drive nine hours alone to Seattle, board a flight for Orlando, and attend a conference about which I knew nothing.

"I've never done anything like this," I blubbered. "I won't know anyone there. I don't know what to expect. And I sense I'm heading into something that's bigger than me!"

"But you believe God wants you to go, right?" said Gene.

"Yes."

"Then go. You won't be alone—He'll be with you. Just take the first step and trust Him to show you what's next."

I wiped my tears, followed Gene's advice, and have never looked back. My writing journey has pushed me far beyond my comfort zone, but that's okay. God has been with me every step of the way. He's given me opportunities I could never have concocted myself.

And although some have made my knees knock with fright, He's always given me the ability and courage I needed to complete the task.

> Whenever Jesus calls someone to get out of the boat, he gives the power to walk on the water. Remember St. Jerome's words: "You command, and immediately the waters are solid." He never calls people to sink. It will surely happen sometimes—but it is not his intent; his call is never a set-up for failure.[6]

Stepping into that unknown future in obedience to God's call guarantees an increased understanding of His power. Just as Peter experienced God's power enabling Him to walk on water, so we experience it in new ways when we leave our comfortable little boat and trust Him with our lives.

Jennifer experiences God's presence and power each day as she presses forward despite her blindness. Theresa is discovering God's power as she learns patience and watches Him open doors for her proposal. I constantly see God's power at work as He enables me to complete writing assignments on time and as He works in women's hearts in response to the Gospel. If I hadn't taken my first fear-filled step, I wouldn't have entered the promised land.

Let me ask you something. Do you sense God prompting you to leave the flatlands and move into unfamiliar territory? Does He want to stretch you, to grow you, to fulfill His ultimate purpose for your life in ways that would boggle your mind? If so, I want to encourage you to remember that His presence is with you. " 'It's all right,' he [Jesus] said. 'I am here! Don't be afraid' " (Matthew 14:27).

Go ahead, sister. Step out and trust Him for the big stuff!

Four Basic Truths

God's timing never ceases to amaze me. As I write this book, my husband and I are facing a transition. We've been involved in a Christian camping ministry in British Columbia for the past decade. Eighteen months ago we began sensing change of some sort coming. We were right!

Six months later, our general director was diagnosed with melanoma. He passed away within the year, leaving the camp's board of directors to appoint his successor. We hoped my husband could assume that role, but God had someone else in mind. We experienced the death of a dream, but as we sifted through our emotions, we sensed God's presence and grew in our understanding of His sovereignty.

We believe God is using these circumstances to lead us to a new assignment, but right now we have lots of unanswered questions: What should we do next? Where will we live? When should we leave? How will relocating affect my speaking ministry? And what will become of our youngest child, who has just been accepted to attend the local community college? If we move away, will she feel as though we're abandoning her?

Several times each day I wonder what tomorrow will bring. I can't say I'm overjoyed to be in this situation, but I *can* say I'm thankful to be dealing with it *at this time*. I'm sequestered in my office, surrounded by books by amazing Christian authors. My Bible lays open before me. As I plow through and ponder materials for this manuscript, my mind is fully absorbed with insights and Scriptures about facing the future without fear.

One overarching theme stands out—God's presence in His followers' lives. In all honesty, this reality empowers me to face our uncertainty with peace rather than panic. I've also found huge consolation in reviewing four other basic truths.

First, God remains steadfast amid life's uncertainties.

What does the future hold? Only heaven knows for sure. Shirley Dobson says, "The future will always be uncertain. While we may enjoy the illusion of safety, even in those moments, we're only a heartbeat away from eternity. That's why we must place our trust in God, knowing 'Jesus Christ is the same yesterday and today and forever' (Hebrews 13:8)."[7]

Life as we know it could change in a split second. It offers no guarantees. That's a scary thought, but we can find comfort in knowing that God never changes. Come flood or fire, He's there to help us navigate the changes.

Second, God cares about the details of our lives.

He rules the course of history, but He also cares about the minute details of our lives. He knows every need. He knows every fear and every tear. "Not even a sparrow, worth only half a penny, can fall to the ground without your Father knowing it. And the very hairs on your head are all numbered. So don't be afraid; you are more valuable to him than a whole flock of sparrows" (Matthew 10:29-30).

Sometimes we don't feel His presence. We may wonder if we've temporarily fallen off His radar. But the truth is, we matter a whole bunch to Him, and He knows exactly what's happening.

Third, God brings good from every trial.

Occasionally our worst fears come to pass. Our hearts break, and we're tempted to question God's sovereignty and sanity. But God is an amazing miracle worker. He's able to take the broken pieces and shape them into something of use and breathtaking beauty. Even when we don't see this happen immediately, we can trust Him to work according to His eternal timetable and for His glory. "And we know that God causes everything to work together for the good of those who love God and are called according to his purpose for them" (Romans 8:28).

Fourth, God always keeps His promises.

Friends with skin on might say things they don't mean or break their promises. But God's words are 100 percent reliable. Because of who He is, lying would be contrary to His nature. With that in mind, we know we can count on Him to do what He says, and that includes delivering us from all our fears. "I prayed to the LORD, and he answered me, freeing me from all my fears" (Psalm 34:4).

Dear reader, these four principles apply to you too. Review them as often as necessary. Thank God several times a day for remaining steadfast, caring about the details of your life, bringing good from every trial, and keeping His promises. Doing so will strengthen your spiritual muscles and bolster your confidence.

And you can take another practical measure to build your courage. I'll sum it up in one word: *remember.*

Remember

The past two decades of my life have been filled with faith-testing opportunities. When I focus on the what-ifs of an uncertain future (just as the ten spies focused on the supersized giants), I grow fearful. But if I look back on the battles I've already won, I gain courage for those that lie ahead.

God knows our fears and that "our perspective of the future is often limited to what we can see now. That's why the refrains of 'remember' and 'do not forget the past' lace the Scriptures together," says one writer.[8]

Do you remember what happened when David the shepherd boy wanted to fight Goliath? His own brothers scoffed at the thought, and King Saul tried to discourage him from doing so. But David recalled the past:

> "I have been taking care of my father's sheep," he said. "When a lion or a bear comes to steal a lamb from the flock, I go after it with a club and take the lamb from its mouth. If the animal turns on me, I catch it by the jaw and club it to death. I have done this to both lions and bears, and I'll do it to this pagan Philistine, too, for he has defied the armies of the living God! The LORD who saved me from the claws of the lion and the bear will save me from this Philistine!" (1 Samuel 17:34-37).

I smile at David's childlike faith. Rather than panicking at what *might* happen, he remembered the victories that God had already accomplished on his behalf. Therein lay his confidence.

Psalm 77 gives us a powerful example of what happens when we recall God's past faithfulness. The first ten verses are filled with despair. They drip with defeat and discouragement. When Asaph, the psalmist, reaches his wits' end, he cries, "I recall all you have done, O LORD; I remember your wonderful deeds of long ago. They are constantly in my thoughts. I cannot stop thinking about them" (Psalm 77:11-12).

At this point, Asaph's tone changes completely! He writes as if he's had a personality transplant. His despair disappears. In its place, we hear proclamations of God as holy and as the worker of wonders and miracles. Asaph acknowledges that God redeemed His people by His strength and led them through the Red Sea. Asaph's gloomy perception of life disappears in light of who God is and what He's done in the past.

Psalm 105 is another example of remembering God's great works in the past. From stories about Joseph in jail to Moses and the manna meals served in the Desert Delicatessen, 45 detailed verses show God's mighty hand actively involved in His children's lives.

Why so much detail? Because we have short and sometimes selective memories. We need constant reminders to keep our focus in the right place, or we slip into bad behavior.

History proves this is true. Each time the Israelites forgot about God's faithfulness, they fell into rebellion, complaining, idolatry, and unbelief. We're no different. When we forget what God has already done, we too fall into unbelief and begin fearing what tomorrow might bring. But recalling God's provision and guidance in the past brings renewed courage and hope for the future.

Katie Brazelton agrees. She spent 14 months seeking employment after being laid off—and she was a single mom. She says she'll be forever grateful to a friend who encouraged her to record examples of God's provisions for her and her kids during that time. "As I began to remember and record God's miracles in my life, I saw how God had been with me all along—just as he promised he would

JOG YOUR MEMORY
WITH JOURNALING

Recalling God's past faithfulness builds courage to face the future. Journaling is a great memory jogger. Here are some basic tips to get you started if you haven't already incorporated this discipline into your life.

- Buy a notebook that fits your budget.

- Commit a few minutes each day to read the Word, pray, and journal. Doing it at the same time each day will help you form the habit.

- Keep your Bible, notebook, and pen in a handy place. I keep mine in a basket beside my favorite chair.

- Write your thoughts about the fear you're struggling with. You might write, "I'm starting a new job next week. I'm afraid of not meeting my employer's expectations. I'm also afraid of the strain that transitioning into a new schedule might place on my family."

- Record a Scripture promise that applies to your situation. For example, "I can do everything with the help of Christ who gives me the strength I need" (Philippians 4:13).

- Turn your thoughts into a prayer using God's Word. *Dear God, I'm afraid of not meeting my employer's expectations in my new job. And I'm scared about the strain this might place on my family as we adjust to the new schedule. But You have promised to give me the strength I need. Thank You that I can do all things through Your power. Amen.*

- Continue praying about this issue, remembering to focus on the Lord rather than your fears.

- Journal your thoughts as the Lord gives you fresh insights and encouragement.

- Record the ways in which the Lord answers your prayers.

- Review your journal periodically. Remembering how the Lord met you in this fear will encourage you when you face another uncertainty.

be. That evidence of God's faithfulness in my life infused me with courage and allowed me to enjoy my new job," she says.[9] I too have found this to be true. As my husband and I wait on the Lord for direction, I can panic or I can pursue peace. I much prefer the latter, but it requires a deliberate effort on my part. It means remembering specific incidents when God met us at a crossroads and guided us to the right decision. He proved Himself faithful then, and because He never changes, I know He'll be faithful to us again. I enjoy inner peace, not panic, by focusing on Him and His unchanging character rather than on the uncertainty of our future.

Surrender

Scripture is sprinkled with stories about ordinary men and women who sacrificed everything for the sake of following God. Their examples show us that they believed Him and trusted Him despite uncertainty. Their hearts were fully surrendered to His purposes, and God used them in extraordinary ways.

Take Mary's example, for instance (Luke 1:26-38). There she was, a teenage girl, engaged to be married to a humble carpenter named Joseph. Her future, as she envisioned it, appeared safe and typical for a girl her age. But things were about to change.

One afternoon the angel Gabriel showed up and flipped her future upside down. "The Lord is with you!" he said. Then he broke some heart-stopping news: Despite the fact that she was still a virgin, Mary was going to become pregnant with God's own child.

Pregnancy out of wedlock in that culture was enough to strike fear into any woman's heart. What would her fiancé think? At the very least, he would divorce her for cheating on him. But what would that matter when public disgrace could lead to a possible stoning? Talk about uncertainty!

Humanly speaking, no one would have blamed Mary if she'd flatly refused to buy into Gabriel's announcement. But she chose a different response. "I am the Lord's servant, and I am willing to accept whatever he wants," she said. "May everything you have said come true."

Whoa! She could have invented a gazillion reasons why Gabriel should visit someone else. Instead, she surrendered her own desires and dreams, embraced God's plan for her life, and willingly trusted Him for the outcome.

What enabled Mary to display a surrendered heart? Perhaps it was her intimate knowledge of God's character as shown in her prayer in Luke 1:46-55. She proclaimed Him as the Mighty One and gave Him credit for doing great things on her behalf. She acknowledged His power, mercy, and faithfulness in fulfilling His promises.

Perhaps it was Gabriel's statement: "The Lord is with you." Knowing that this mighty God was walking with her into the unknown brought courage to deal with whatever lay ahead.

The same is true for you.

Whatever your fears, whatever the unknowns or the challenges in your life, God has promised to provide for you, to share His pleasure with you, to protect you, and to give you His enduring presence.

The fact remains that when we sign the blank contract of surrender, there are no guarantees about where God will lead us or how difficult our journey will be. Yet we know the character of the One in whom we've placed our trust. And we know that God's promises more than offset any risks or dangers or challenges that He may allow into our lives.[10]

What will tomorrow bring? God knows. And He'll be with us. What more do we need?

+ POINTS FOR PROGRESS +

The LORD is my light and my salvation—
    so why should I be afraid?
The LORD protects me from danger—
    so why should I tremble?

When evil people come to destroy me,
> when my enemies and foes attack me,
> they will stumble and fall.
Though a mighty army surrounds me,
> my heart will know no fear.
Even if they attack me,
> I remain confident (Psalm 27:1-3).

1. According to these verses, what's the basis for our confidence despite frightening circumstances?

2. Explain the significance of the statement "The LORD is my light" in view of a future that sometimes looms big and black.

3. Sometimes we base our confidence in objects of false security. Name several. Why is the Lord our only hope for protection?

4. God doesn't always deliver us from harm. What Scripture promise can we claim when He allows us to suffer?

5. Describe a situation in which you feared something in the future. What effect did that have on your outlook toward life? How did God meet you in the midst of that fear?

✦ PROMISES TO PONDER ✦

For you are my hiding place;
> you protect me from trouble.
> You surround me with songs of victory.
The LORD says, "I will guide you along the best pathway
> for your life.
> I will advise you and watch over you"…
For the word of the LORD holds true,
> and everything he does is worthy of our trust.

He loves whatever is just and good,
   and his unfailing love fills the earth
(Psalm 32:7-8; 33:4-5).

I prayed to the LORD, and he answered me,
   freeing me from all my fears.
Those who look to him for help will be radiant with joy;
   no shadow of shame will darken their faces.
I cried out to the LORD in my suffering and he heard me.
   He set me free from all my fears…
Taste and see that the LORD is good.
   Oh, the joys of those who trust in him!
(Psalm 34:4-6,8).

"For I know the plans I have for you," says the LORD. "They are plans for good and not for disaster, to give you a future and a hope. In those days when you pray, I will listen. If you look for me in earnest, you will find me when you seek me. I will be found by you," says the LORD (Jeremiah 29:11-14).

✦ PRAYING THE PROMISES ✦

Father, I praise You because You are the perfect hiding place. Thank You for promising to protect me from trouble and surrounding me with songs of victory. Thank You for promising to guide me along the best pathway for my life, for advising me, and for watching over me. I praise You for keeping Your promises and being worthy of my trust. Open my eyes to see evidences of Your unfailing love that fills the earth. Amen.

Dear God, only You can free me from all my fears. Hear me when I cry to You. Make my face radiant with joy! Let no shadow darken my countenance. When I am afraid of what tomorrow might bring, please allow me to experience You— to taste and see Your goodness at work on my behalf. Thank You for the joy that comes from trusting You. Amen.

O Lord, I surrender to Your plans for my life. I don't know what they are, but I know they're good, designed to give me a future and a hope. Thank You for promising to listen when I pray. Thank You for promising to let me find You if I seek for You. I love You and rest in Your goodness. Amen.

6

Who, Me?

Fear imprisons, faith liberates; fear paralyzes,
faith empowers; fear disheartens, faith encourages;
fear sickens, faith heals; fear makes useless,
faith makes serviceable.

HARRY EMERSON FOSDICK

If God is who He says He is, why am I afraid? The question nagged me while I folded laundry and prepared meals. It pestered me as I typed. It haunted me when I closed my eyes at night. I could neither escape nor answer it. And believe me, I tried.

Write a book about the fears that women face, a quiet voice had whispered a year prior.

Who, me? I'd asked. *No way. I'm just a housewife who's written a few magazine articles and one devotional book. What do I know about writing a chapter book like that?*

Just do it, the voice persisted.

The idea terrified me. *I'll never find enough words to fill 250 pages!*

Trust Me, the voice prodded.

Fear engulfed me, and I groped for an excuse. *I...uh...I don't have time!*

Make time.

Aw, c'mon. This is too big for me, I whimpered. *What if...* I paused

for a moment, not wanting to say the four-letter word. *What if...
I...fail?*

Trust Me.

You'd think God's assurance would outweigh my misgivings.
Not in this case. I was plain ol' deaf. And dumb. I pursued other
activities, promising to write the book after I'd finished the next
project, and the next, and the next. A year passed, during which
time God tried catching my attention several times.

You know how He does that, right? A pastor's sermon makes
you certain he's been spying on you. A Scripture verse leaps off the
page and into your heart. A quote reads as though it was custom
designed for you. I knew what God was up to, but I played stupid.
My fear of inadequacy paralyzed me, and I refused to budge. *Sorry,
God, You're talking to the wrong woman.*

Have you ever spoken those words to God? Perhaps you've sensed
Him asking you to step far beyond your comfort zone. He's assigned
you a task that takes you beyond your training. *Who, me?* you've
said. *You must be joking.* But deep down in your heart, you know
He's serious. And that scares you just as it did me.

The fear of inadequacy looms large before us, but it's nothing
new. More than three thousand years ago, Moses felt it too (Exodus
3:1–4:17).

A Moses Moment

The morning dawned like any other for Moses as he tended his
father-in-law's sheep, but it didn't remain ho-hum for long. The
burning bush was the first clue that something unique was about to
happen. When the bush starting talking, Moses sensed a straight-
up learning curve hurtling his way. He was right.

"Hey, Moses," God boomed. "I have an assignment for you.
I'm coming to rescue My people from the Egyptians. And I'm
appointing *you* as executive director of the exodus plan."

"Me? You're talking to the wrong guy." Moses laughed nervously,
but something told him this was no comedy. "I'm just a nobody—

how could I possibly appear before Pharaoh? And how could I even hope to lead the Israelites from Egypt?"

"I will be with you," said God.

You'd think God's promise would have overcome Moses' misgivings, but no. Despite God's reassurance, Moses argued with Him and expressed his doubts. Who could blame the poor guy? After all, tending a flock of sheep was one thing. Defying Pharaoh and assuming responsibility for an entire nation's well-being was another.

In modern-day terms, that would be like driving for the school carpool one day and being assigned to direct NASA's space shuttle program the next. Or being asked to host a national TV show about landscaping when the only green thing you've grown is mold on the month-old bread in your cupboard. Who *wouldn't* feel inadequate?

As Moses stood beside that burning bush, listening to God's voice, he focused on his felt inadequacies. "O Lord, I'm just not a good speaker. I never have been, and I'm not now, even after You have spoken to me. I'm clumsy with words."

"Trust Me," God replied. "I'll help you speak. I'll teach you what to say. I'll enable you to do mighty miracles to prove that I've appointed you."

But this is where Moses, prisoner of the fear of inadequacy, pushed the limits. "Lord, please! Send someone else!" he begged.

And God became angry. He had big plans for His people, and He wanted to include Moses in the adventure. He'd promised His presence and He'd promised to equip him, but Moses didn't believe.

God would change Pharaoh's heart. *God* would supply food and water for the masses. *God* would part the Red Sea. He simply wanted Moses to say, "Sure thing, God. I'll do whatever You say. I trust You!" But Moses couldn't see beyond inadequacy and possible failure.

Thankfully, God didn't write off Moses as a wimp. He heard Moses' concerns. He understood his fear, and He gave him everything necessary to get the job done.

Thankfully, God didn't write me off when I argued with Him about this book. He heard my concerns, He understood my fear. And one morning, in my kitchen, He met me in the midst of them.

Who Do You Think I Am?

During the year that I played deaf and dumb, Gene and I had been studying the book *Experiencing God* by Henry Blackaby. One morning several weeks into the course, I sat at my kitchen table preparing the week's lesson. The lesson addressed the "crisis of belief"—a new concept for me. One statement flew off the page: "Anytime God leads you to do something that has God-sized dimensions, you will face a crisis of belief. When you face a crisis of belief, what you do next reveals what you really believe about God."[1]

The Holy Spirit used those words to flood my head and heart with the light of truth. I recalled writing my first book a year prior and wrestling with the fear of inadequacy every day during that process. I also recalled the exhilaration I felt upon its completion, and I watched in wide-eyed wonder as God began using it to change women's lives. He'd equipped me for that task then, but for whatever reason, I doubted His ability to do it again.

Recognizing my unbelief as an insult to God, I began to weep. The God of the universe wanted to trust me with a God-sized assignment, but I'd brushed Him off with a simple *No thanks. Not interested. Not capable.* I'd argued with Him for an entire year! And that response revealed my belief about Him—I thought He was too small to accomplish the task through me. He'd equipped me for writing the first book, but for some strange reason, He'd shrunk since then. He just *couldn't* equip me now.

The truth hurt. Tears flowed. *I'm so sorry, God,* I said. *Forgive my sin of unbelief and grant me faith instead.*

The Holy Spirit's gentle voice nudged me. *Who do you think I am? If you believe I'm truly God, then do what I say. Just trust Me.*

I considered His words. I weighed my options—obey or disobey. And I made my choice.

Okay, God. If You really want me to write a book about the fears that women face, I'll do it. I haven't got a clue how to accomplish this, but I trust You. Relief and a twinge of excitement replaced the fear I'd wrestled for so long.

Henry Blackaby says, "When you obey God, He will accomplish through you what He has purposed to do. When God does something through your life that only He can do, you will come to know Him more intimately. If you do not obey, you will miss out on some of the most exciting experiences of your life."[2]

Dr. Blackaby is right! Because I said yes, I've come to know God's enabling power more intimately. I've experienced physical strength to sit at the computer for hours each day. I've witnessed His sovereignty as He's brought specific women across my path at just the right time. I've known His peace throughout the writing process, even in the midst of a hectic summer camp schedule. And I've felt His delight as I've expressed my dependence on Him day by day. My only regret is that I didn't say yes earlier.

God wants to accomplish great things through His children's lives. He extends an invitation: *Hey, My dear daughter—I have an assignment for you!* Too often, though, the fear of inadequacy wraps its chains around our hearts and we say, *No thanks. You're asking the wrong woman.* If that's our response, we miss out on faith-building adventures that surpass our wildest imaginations. But when we say yes, we experience God Himself and the deep-seated joy that comes from walking in harmony with Him.

Fear Breeders

We live in a climate that brings rain and lots of it. Combined with mild temperatures, our area boasts a perfect place for plants to thrive. In fact, our ivy is so big, it looks as though someone has been feeding it steroids. That's both good and bad.

On the positive side, the ivy is beautiful to behold as it curls and winds its way up the rock wall lining our yard. On the negative side, it can be destructive, completely hiding the rock wall and choking other plants if left unchecked.

Like our ivy, the fear of inadequacy carries both a positive and a negative aspect. On the positive side, it can be the tool that brings us into a greater understanding of God's power at work within us. It can result in our seeing God do amazing things far beyond our imaginations. When we acknowledge our fear and say yes to God in spite of it, we grow in character and confidence. The result is beautiful to behold!

On the negative side, the fear of inadequacy can take control of our hearts and minds if we allow it to. It can choke our potential and render us useless. We need to be on our guard and take action lest it overtake us. To prevent the fear of inadequacy from becoming a destructive force in our lives, let's recognize several factors that breed its growth.

The Fear of Making Mistakes

Someone once said, "The biggest mistake you can make is continually fearing you will make one." How true!

The fear of making mistakes can hold women hostage. If we allow it to persist, it prevents us from expressing our opinions, learning new skills, and honing our abilities. It robs us of personal fulfillment and joy, and it denies the world of our insights and giftedness. This recent e-mail shows you what I'm talking about:

> Fear is a gripping force that can hinder us from stepping out in faith. Today I am (again) struggling with my role as women's ministry leader. Am I really a leader? Am I the one for this job? Bottom line...FEAR!!! I want to do what God wants but I'm so afraid of making mistakes.

Perhaps this gal has terrific ideas for retreat themes. Maybe she has a vision for older women mentoring younger women. Perhaps she'd love to lead a Bible study. But fear tells her that she might make a mistake. A little inner voice taunts, *You can't do this job. You're not equipped. Your ideas are silly. If you share them with anyone, you'll be laughed at or misunderstood.* She longs to step out and make a difference, but the fear of making a mistake tells her not to. *You'd best not take a risk because you might…heaven forbid…fail.*

A magazine article written by a different woman echoes the same struggle:

> My faith was greatly lacking when it came to trusting God to take care of my life, so I lived in fear much of the time. If someone asked me why I didn't do a certain thing, my reply would often start with, "I'm afraid that I won't do it right" or "I'm afraid of what people might say."[3]

Boy, can I relate! After living nearly three years in Nepal, Gene and I settled in Washington state. We attended a church that included four or five pianists in a rotating schedule. For two years I silently wished I could join the rotation, but I felt rusty after not playing piano during our overseas stay. I'd convinced myself that I would make multiple mistakes if I tried. I didn't want others to think of me as an incompetent klutz, so I kept my mouth shut.

One Sunday after church, the pastor's wife approached me. "I hear that you play piano," she said with a smile. "Would you like to join the rotation?"

I panicked. *Who told her?* Then I saw my husband's guilty grin. "I'll think about it," I replied.

The drive home proved my suspicions. "Why did you tell her?" I demanded.

"Because it's time you use your skills," he answered. "You've been hiding long enough." He was right. And I was scared silly. Nevertheless, I agreed to adding my name to the list.

Fear engulfed me each time my Sunday approached. Playing piano was a stressor, not an act of worship. One morning, the pastor took his place on the platform a minute or so before my prelude's conclusion. The people had been visiting, but when he sat down, a hush fell across the congregation. I panicked. *Oh no! Now people will hear me play. I'd better add a fancy ending!*

My fingers shook, but I managed something acceptable. Then came the last note. I hit the key with extra oomph. Trouble was…it was the wrong note! I tried again. Wrong note! I hate to admit it, but I tried a third time. If I'd had a white flag, I would have waved it wildly at that point.

Embarrassed, I glanced at the pastor. He threw me a mile-wide grin. I was nearly dying from humiliation, but I returned a forced smile. I figured that was more appropriate than bursting into tears.

No one mentioned my boo-boo when the service ended. They'd probably already forgotten, but I hadn't. I crawled home, convinced that I'd disgraced myself and would never do that again.

Thankfully, God gave me a husband with a healthier perspective. "So you made a mistake? I'll bet no one even noticed." Gene gave me a hug. "Next time, don't worry about what other people think. Just play for the Lord and enjoy yourself."

I heeded his advice. A couple weeks later, I climbed back onto that piano bench and played again. This time, my focus was in the right place.

I've never become a concert pianist, but over the years I've gained a little wisdom: Mistakes don't signal the end of the world. Neither do they lessen our worth in God's eyes. They do, however, offer opportunities to learn and grow.

Someone said, "Many people choose safe lives in which failure (and, therefore, real success) is highly unlikely. They never take risks, and they never fail; but they also die without any real service. They may never make a mistake, but they'll also never make a difference."[4]

Do you want to make a difference? Then be willing to take a risk. Don't let the fear of making a mistake deny you the joy and fulfillment of living life to the full. If you're afraid of making a mistake, ask the Lord to help you face that fear. Ask Him to show

Himself strong in your weakness. Then move forward, resolved to do your best, and let Him do the rest. As Donna Partow says, "We don't have to be afraid of losing God's approval when we stumble and fall. He who calls us to run the race is the one who helps us over the finish line."[5]

The Fear of Not Measuring Up

The fear of inadequacy grips women young and old alike. These comments show the struggle:

> As a newly married woman, I don't know if I'm fulfilling my duties as well as good wives ought to.

> I don't think I'm a good mom. My children aren't as well behaved as my friends' kids. Sometimes I fear scarring my kids for life.

> On the outside, I look like an organized woman. But— don't laugh!—if you came to my house, you'd see the real me. My house is a mess, and I'm afraid others will discover who I really am. I'm just *not* as organized as most people.

> I've been asked to sing in church, and I'm afraid to say yes. I don't think I'm as capable as other singers.

> Sometimes I agree when people ask me to do certain tasks. But then I second-guess myself. *How will I be able to do the job? Why did I say yes when other women have a lot more talent?*

These comments reveal a common thread—each speaker has fallen into the trap of comparison. She's measuring herself against an invisible standard of behavior or performance and expressing her fear of not measuring up.

We often fall into the comparison trap with our physical appearance as well. Magazines, movies, and television flaunt skinny models and actresses with silky hair, gorgeous skin, and flawless makeup. For those who fall short of that standard, department stores sell cosmetics that mask blemishes, deodorants and perfumes that cover unpleasant odors, and dyes that color graying hair.

And, oh yes, the fashion market devises little tricks to hide our figure flaws. Vertical stripes make us appear streamlined. Thigh-length jackets disguise bumps and bulges. Capri pants cover the evidence of too many ice cream treats.

If we're not on guard, the comparison trap can catch and lock us in green-eyed envy. We look in the mirror, shrug, and think, *I have nothing to offer.* We focus on our perceived shortcomings rather than the living God, whose Holy Spirit dwells within us. And then we retreat, feeling less pretty or less productive or less promising.

When that happens, we never realize our potential in Christ or the fullness of His power that works within us. As John Ortberg says, we bury the treasure God has given us.

Ortberg shares other wise words about the comparison trap too:

> I must ruthlessly refuse to compare my talents with anyone else. Comparison will lead to pride and a false sense of superiority if I'm ahead of someone, and misery if I'm behind. Or worse, I will discount and bury the irreplaceable treasure that the Lord of the Gift has given to me alone...I must come to identify, cultivate, invest, prize, and enjoy the gifts that have been given to me. The Lord of the Gift is very wise. He knew exactly what he was doing when he created you. He is well-pleased that you exist. He has entrusted to you everything you need to fulfill the purpose for which you were created.[6]

You have unique gifts, and so do I. Perhaps your musical abilities lead others to worship God through song. Maybe your culinary skills bless shut-ins or those who visit your home. Perhaps your teaching skills instill a love for reading in children. Or you're a natural with seniors. Or with immigrants who need practical help with grocery shopping and language learning. Maybe you're a whiz with crunching numbers and balancing budgets. Or you have a knack for listening to those who need a listening ear.

God has wired each of us in a unique way for a unique purpose. He's designed a potpourri of personalities and gifts! Each one is necessary for God's kingdom to function and grow as it ought. Embracing that truth sets us free to be the women He made us to be.

Several things happen when we forego comparisons and, instead, embrace our uniqueness. First, as Donna Partow says, "When you run the race God intended for you to run, you suddenly tap into his unlimited power. You tap into a reservoir of strength, wisdom, and enthusiasm that was completely unavailable to you as long as you were 'doing your own thing.'"[7]

In other words, we experience God's enabling when we concentrate on the work He has assigned us rather than worrying about the possibility of another woman doing a better job, or wishing we had someone else's skills.

Second, we experience contentment with who we are. We stop wishing we had another's singing ability or sense of humor. We start appreciating the way God designed us, and we realize the importance of our role in building His kingdom.

And third, embracing our uniqueness enables us to encourage others without feeling threatened or intimidated by their success. God has a plan for us, and He has a plan for them. We should feel honored to have a role in promoting His purposes even if we must take a backseat and applaud their success.

Pride

Two revival ministers visited our church several years ago. They preached the Word of God nightly for approximately two weeks, and the Holy Spirit moved in mighty ways as people confessed sin and made restitution wherever necessary.

During those meetings, the topic of pride came up repeatedly.

That's when I first heard that low self-esteem is simply a form of inverted pride. That thought grabbed my attention! I wanted to say, "Wait a minute! Take it easy on those of us who struggle with a sense of inadequacy. We have enough stuff to contend with already—don't lay a guilt trip on us too." But as time went on, I understood the connection.

You see, pride results when I become mesmerized with *me*. I want to protect myself from anything that might bring harm or injury to my ego, so I avoid situations that might result in embarrassment or humiliation. I decline opportunities to make a difference because I might make a mistake and give others reason to laugh at me. Rather than admit my inadequacy and trust God to look after me, I say, *I can't,* and run the other way.

Call it low self-esteem if you like. But in essence, it's simply an elevated sense of *me* that says, *I can't do this. God wants to give me a special task, and He's told me that He'll equip me, but I don't believe Him.*

Pam Farrel says that one of the ugliest sins she ever had to confess was pride:

> I caught myself wondering how I could be guilty of pride, since so often I battle a self-confidence problem. Then God pointed out that oversensitive low self-esteem is pride inside out. When I battle low self-esteem, I am still focusing on me. I am concentrating on seeking approval and encouragement. My eyes are on my needs, while God wants my eyes on him.[8]

Humility, on the other hand, willingly admits inadequacy and embraces God's sufficiency. Its attitude says, *You want to use me? I'm honored. I can't do this task, but I know You can. And I look forward to experiencing You more intimately through it. Thank You for loving me enough to trust me.*

Pride breeds the fear of inadequacy, and God wants to set us free from its power in our lives. That happens when we admit our inadequacies and release our desire to control our circumstances and destiny. A.W. Tozer explains this more fully:

> To men and women everywhere Jesus says, "Come unto me, and I will give you rest." The rest He offers is the rest of meekness, the blessed relief which comes when we accept ourselves for what we are and cease to pretend. It will take some courage at first, but the needed grace will come as we learn that we are sharing this new and easy yoke with the strong Son of God Himself. He calls it "my yoke," and He walks at one end while we walk at the other.[9]

Aaahhh—sweet, sweet rest. When we acknowledge our weaknesses and inadequacies, we no longer have to hide behind a facade lest others find out who we really are. Admitting our inadequacies isn't easy, but Christ helps us do so. He's opposed to the proud but gives grace to the humble. And when our hearts have been humbled, exciting things happen.

Humble Helena

Meet my friend Helena—an 82-year-old widow whose life models true humility. She possesses no formal training in business administration or social work. She doesn't own a big bank account. Her only credential is that her heart belongs completely to God.

Born in Russia, Helena and her family fled persecution in 1929. Terror-filled nighttime travels produced a lifelong fear of the dark. The family escaped to Canada, but they lived in poverty and ate a skimpy diet. As a result, Helena acquired rickets, and walking became a challenge. Poor eyesight meant wearing thick glasses.

"I thought I was so ugly that I felt sorry for anyone who looked at me," Helena says. "I refused to look in a mirror when I combed my hair because I didn't want to see myself. I didn't think I had anything to offer anyone."

If anyone had reason to hide behind her felt inadequacies, Helena did. But beneath the battered self-worth lay a heart committed to God and a desire to serve Him in Africa. Helena applied to a mission agency upon graduation from Bible college but was rejected for health reasons. She approached a second agency. Again she received the response, "Don't bother applying."

Helena married and raised three children. When she was widowed at age 70, she asked God, "What do You want me to do with the rest of my life?" The answer came: "Preach the Gospel."

Helena sold her belongings. Several months later, she set foot on African soil, healthier than she'd ever been. She helped establish a library for pastors and teachers, founded three feeding centers for hungry children, and started an orphanage for Kenyan street kids.

Every spring she packs her bags, purchases a plane ticket, and travels alone to Nairobi to visit the orphanage. "I was just a poor farm girl with many health problems," says Helena with a chuckle, "but that didn't matter to God. He uses and equips anyone who's willing to be used."[10]

Humble Helena. When I grow up, I want to be just like her. (Actually, why wait?) Her life models gentle humility but boasts an unswerving faith in God's power and His ability to use whomever He chooses. Has she made mistakes in her endeavors? Oh, yes. She's learned by trial and error many times over. But she's never allowed the fear of making another mistake to prevent her from trying again. Has she struggled with the fear of not measuring up? Oh, yes. And the mission boards' rejections didn't exactly help her in that department.

But today, Helena has shed the facade and admitted her inadequacies. Her focus is on the right person—Christ—and on His desire and ability to make a difference through a yielded life.

> Remember, dear brothers and sisters, that few of you were wise in the world's eyes, or powerful, or wealthy when God called you. Instead, God deliberately chose things

the world considers foolish in order to shame those who think they are wise. And he chose those who are powerless to shame those who are powerful. God chose things despised by the world, things counted as nothing at all, and used them to bring to nothing what the world considers important, so that no one can ever boast in the presence of God (1 Corinthians 1:26-29).

Paul explained it well, didn't he? God doesn't necessarily call the equipped; He equips the called. Therefore, we can't use our inadequacies as excuses for not participating with Him! He chooses us to show His glory through us. When there's no human explanation for what's happening, unbelievers sit up and take notice. Believers pay attention. And God receives the glory. When we refuse to cooperate, we deny Him that opportunity.

So what are our options? We can choose to say, *I can't.* Or we can trust Him and say, *In Your strength, I can do whatever You ask me to do.* People who have wholeheartedly followed God—as Helena has—can tell you that doing so won't always feel safe or comfortable, but they'll also tell you that there's no better way to experience Him.

So, my dear...

Who, me?

Yes...YOU! Let's take a peek at some practical steps to conquering the fear of inadequacy.

Conquering Fear

"So how does one go about obtaining the faith that conquers fear? Ironically, it is by refusing to pretend. It is by admitting to God that we are terrified and we aren't sure we have enough faith for the battle," says Rebecca Manley Pippert.[11]

Telling God how we feel is the first step, and one that shouldn't intimidate us. Our confession comes as no surprise—He already knows our secret thoughts. He wants us to be real, to be honest. To

NO MORE EXCUSES!

Talk about timely! This tidbit showed up in my inbox as I was writing this chapter. It had been forwarded from a forward without naming the original source. If you know the original source, please let me know. Enjoy!

The next time you feel as if God can't use you, just remember…

Noah was a drunk	Abraham was too old
Isaac was a daydreamer	Jacob was a liar
Leah was ugly	Joseph was abused
Moses had a stuttering problem	Gideon was afraid
Samson was a womanizer	Rahab was a prostitute
Jeremiah and Timothy were too young	Isaiah preached naked
David was an adulterer and a murderer	Elijah was suicidal
Jonah ran from God	Naomi was a widow
Job went bankrupt	Peter denied Christ
The disciples fell asleep while praying	Zaccheus was too small
Martha worried about everything	Paul was too religious
Timothy had an ulcer	Lazarus was dead!

The Samaritan woman was divorced—more than once

Now—no more excuses!

---

confide in Him as our closest friend. To holler for help and expect Him to rush to our rescue when we're in way over our heads.

> Whether God speaks or not, His existence is clearly evident in everything I see, and today He gently reminded me that I am in control of almost nothing at all. I can only choose to trust Him and acknowledge the truth that I am frail and embarrassingly small. Only God through

His own strength and power will enable me to fulfill His call. And He will, you know—if I continue on this journey called believe.[12]

The other day while reading my Bible, I came across an Old Testament passage that beautifully illustrates this. There was a war going on...again. The armies of Reuben, Gad, and Manasseh had 44,760 warriors. *Skilled* warriors, they were—well-prepared for combat and armed with shields, swords, and bows. But when these fellows came against the "ites"—the Hagrites, Jeturites, Naphishites, and the Nodabites—they suddenly felt frail and embarrassingly small.

Rather than retreat and hide, however, they hollered for help. "They cried out to God during the battle, and he answered their prayer because they trusted in him. So the Hagrites and all their allies were defeated...many of the Hagrites were killed in the battle because God was fighting against them" (1 Chronicles 5:18-20,22).

Why did God rush to rescue the warriors? Not because they dropped to their knees, prayed eloquently, and went through a bunch of religious rituals. He answered because they were real and they trusted in Him.

Admitting our fear to God comes first. After that, we need to move ahead. The armies of Reuben, Gad, and Manasseh didn't cry for help and then sit still. They prayed and kept fighting.

Aristotle said that "courage is not the absence of fear, but the ability to operate in the face of fear." Remember 9/11? Think for a moment about the rescue workers who entered the Twin Towers after terrorists crashed two airliners into the buildings. Despite the fear of danger to their own lives, these men and women displayed courage by entering the flaming buildings. That's how God wants us to respond to God-sized tasks—by acknowledging our fear to Him and then moving into action.

My friend Gwen did this, but it wasn't easy. She struggled with the fear of inadequacy from her childhood, but she'd masked those feelings with an air of confidence. When her church decided to start a Christian school, her pastor asked her to teach kindergarten, based solely upon her experience as a teacher's aide. "Sure, I can do that," she said, hiding behind her veneer.

But fear gripped her as the beginning of the school year approached. Gwen sunk into a spiritual pit. Panicked, she told the pastor, "I don't think I can do this job."

The pastor—wise man—prayed with Gwen and then asked her to pray about it for several days. He promised that he and his wife would pray too, and he asked her to return to his office a few days later.

Gwen followed the pastor's counsel. She poured out her heart to God, and He answered with Proverbs 3:5-6: "Trust in the LORD with all your heart; do not depend on your own understanding. Seek his will in all you do, and he will direct your paths."

Trust in Me, the Holy Spirit said. *Don't trust in yourself. Without Me, you don't have what it takes in any situation. I am your peace, your strength, your wisdom, your discernment, your love. Be still.*

When Gwen visited the pastor again, he assured her that if she took the job, the school and church staff would support her. His words encouraged her to take the risk. And when she did, God proved His ability to use her despite her felt inadequacies.[13]

John Ortberg says, "Fear has created more practicing heretics than bad theology ever has, for it makes us live as though we serve a limited, finite, partially present, semi-competent God. You will never know God is trustworthy if you don't risk obeying him."[14]

Gwen found those words to be true. She risked obeying God despite her fear, and to this day, she's thankful she did! If she'd listened to her fear and refused to budge, she would have missed the opportunity to see God equip her and bless the kindergartners through her. And not only that, but she would not have known the freedom that came when she shed her mask of self-confidence.

Another important step in overcoming our fear of inadequacy is to read the Word of God. It's filled with declarations of what He's like:

- powerful (Psalm 76)
- holy (Psalm 99:3)
- eternal and unchanging (Psalm 102:27)
- slow to get angry; merciful, gracious (Psalm 103:8)
- filled with unfailing love toward those who fear Him (Psalm 103:11)
- tender and compassionate to those who fear Him (Psalm 103:13)
- robed with honor and majesty (Psalm 104:1)

The God we serve is very much alive and well! And He's much bigger and more powerful and amazing than our peewee minds will ever comprehend! We understand more and more about God's character as we familiarize ourselves with stories that reveal His faithfulness to past generations. We bolster our courage when we memorize His promises. Fear subsides when we allow God's thoughts to penetrate our minds and transform our thoughts. And it shrivels when we turn those thoughts back to Him in praise, even if we do it by the sheer act of our will.

Gideon felt frail and embarrassingly small when God told him to save the Israelites from the Midianites. *Who, me?* he thought. "How can I rescue Israel? My clan is the weakest in the whole tribe of Manasseh, and I am the least in my entire family!" (Judges 6:15). But his attitude immediately changed when he recognized God's true identity. He left his hiding place and became a mighty man of valor.

That's how it is with us too. By reading the Word of God, we learn more about who He is. That knowledge gives us faith to believe His promises, and when we obey Him by faith, we experience who He is. We can leave our hiding places and become mighty women of valor.

Who, Me? A Woman of Valor?

Regardless of your age or stage in life, God is calling you to be a mighty woman of valor. He's not looking for perfect people to fill His ranks. If *that* were the case, we'd all be sent to the end of the line. Rather, He's looking for folks whose hearts are completely yielded to Him. "The eyes of the LORD search the whole earth in order to strengthen those whose hearts are fully committed to him," says 2 Chronicles 16:9.

What characterizes these people? They love God's Word and enjoy a growing relationship with Him. They obey His commands and trust His ability to equip them for the task He's assigned. They move forward even when their knees are knocking, and they're fueled by focusing on His adequacies rather than on their inadequacies. They're the ones who God wants in His ranks, and He's promised to strengthen them!

Perhaps you're not so sure. You're in a new job and feeling like a misfit. You're taking college classes and feeling like a preschooler again. Your husband has left you to raise your kids alone. An elderly parent needs round-the-clock care. You're a new mom, and you're exhausted from walking the floor all night with a colicky baby.

"I can't do this!" you cry.

Yes, you can. Just take care of first things first. God has promised to strengthen those whose hearts are fully His. Cry out to Him, admit your need for help, and expect Him to see you through.

I want to end this chapter with a quote that beautifully summarizes everything we've talked about. Read it. Ponder it. And take it to heart, dear sister.

> Self-confidence takes a little inventory to see what our internal resources are. Then, based on that self-evaluation, you come to some conclusions about what you can or cannot do. Self-confidence looks inward.
>
> God-Confidence looks upward. God-Confidence realizes that it doesn't matter whether or not you're qualified; what matters is whether or not God has called you...

If God is calling you to do something, take courage and do it with quiet confidence. "Trust in the Lord with all thine heart; and lean not unto thine own understanding. In all thy ways acknowledge him, and he shall direct thy paths" (Proverbs 3:5-6).[15]

✦ POINTS FOR PROGRESS ✦

The New Testament missionary Paul says that he was given a thorn in the flesh to keep him from getting proud. We don't know what this thorn was, although some historians believe it was either malaria, epilepsy, or an eye disease. Whatever it was, it sometimes kept him from working. On three occasions he asked God to remove it from him, but God said no. Paul's response is recorded in 2 Corinthians 12:9-10:

> Each time he [God] said, "My gracious favor is all you need. My power works best in your weakness." So now I am glad to boast about my weaknesses, so that the power of Christ may work through me. Since I know it is all for Christ's good, I am quite content with my weaknesses and with insults, hardships, persecutions, and calamities. For when I am weak, then I am strong.

1. Some folks with chronic physical ailments might consider themselves inadequate to fulfill a God-given assignment. What was Paul's perspective?

2. God is fully aware of our supposed limitations, but that doesn't hinder Him from wanting to use us to build His kingdom. What does He say is the only thing we really need in order to fulfill the tasks He gives us?

3. God says, "My power works best in your weakness." Describe a situation in which you felt inadequate for a

task. How did you witness God's power at work despite your weakness?

4. John 15:5 says, "Apart from me [Christ] you can do nothing." Compare this with Philippians 4:13 which says, "I can do everything with the help of Christ who gives me the strength I need." According to these verses, on what or on whom are we to depend? To what degree must we rely on Him to perform any God-given task effectively?

5. Write a prayer to God. If you struggle with the sin of unbelief, confess it. Then thank Him for His gracious favor in your life. Thank Him for equipping you with His power for any task He assigns.

✦ PROMISES TO PONDER ✦

"To whom will you compare me? Who is my equal?" asks the Holy One. Look up into the heavens. Who created all the stars? He brings them out one after another, calling each by its name. And he counts them to see that none are lost or have strayed away…Don't you know that the LORD is the everlasting God, the Creator of all the earth? He never grows faint or weary. No one can measure the depths of his understanding. He gives power to those who are tired and worn out; he offers strength to the weak. Even youths will become exhausted, and young men will give up. But those who wait on the LORD will find new strength. They will fly high on wings like eagles. They will run and not grow weary. They will walk and not faint (Isaiah 40:25-26,28-31).

I can do everything with the help of Christ who gives me the strength I need (Philippians 4:13).

There is no one like the God of Israel.
He rides across the heavens to help you,
across the skies in majestic splendor.
The eternal God is your refuge,
and his everlasting arms are under you
(Deuteronomy 33:26-27).

But as for you, Israel, my servant, Jacob my chosen one, descended from my friend Abraham, I have called you back from the ends of the earth so you can serve me. For I have chosen you and will not throw you away. Don't be afraid, for I am with you. Do not be dismayed, for I am your God. I will strengthen you. I will help you. I will uphold you with my victorious right hand (Isaiah 41:8-10).

✦ PRAYING THE PROMISES ✦

Dear God, no one compares to You. You created the stars, and You call them each by name. You count them so none are lost. No one else can do this! You alone are mighty and powerful! I praise You because You never grow weak or tired. When I'm frazzled and feeling totally inadequate for my tasks, please remind me that Your limitless, almighty power is at work within me. As I wait on You, please renew my strength as the eagles'. Amen.

Father, I praise You because You are unique! Thank You for promising to ride across the heavens to help me. Thank You for being my refuge forever and for holding me in Your everlasting arms. Your greatness gives me the strength to do everything—absolutely everything—You ask me to do. Grant me the faith to believe this is true. Amen.

Dear God, thank You for choosing me to be Your child and servant. I'm honored that You want a relationship with me and have included me in Your eternal plans. Thank You for understanding my fearful heart. Thank You for promising to be with me and to give me strength. I believe Your words and trust that You will help me and hold me up with Your victorious right hand. Amen.

7

Will You Love *the* Real Me?

*The cave you fear to enter
holds the treasure you seek.*

JOSEPH CAMPBELL

"I can hardly wait for tomorrow! How about you?" whispered one of my college girlfriends as the professor began his lecture. I smiled and nodded, thankful that the clock cut our conversation short.

Less than 24 hours remained before the senior class would vacate the Bible college campus for its long-awaited annual retreat. The event, held about six weeks prior to graduation, was the last hurrah—a time to trade textbooks for table games, hikes, singing, laughter, and fireside testimonies. *Everyone* was pumped and had already started packing their bags. Everyone, that is, but me.

I couldn't go. I just *couldn't*. And so I made an alternate plan. No one knew, and I wasn't about to tell—at least not until the timing was right.

The girls' dorm fairly buzzed with excitement the next morning. That's when I put my plan into action. Faking illness, I told my friends to enjoy their weekend, and then I checked myself into the campus infirmary.

"But Grace, you can't miss this," they pleaded. "This is the

151

biggest weekend of the whole year. It's the last time our class will be together. After graduation, we'll all go different directions and never see each other again. Please come. You can rest there."

They tried their best to change my mind, but it was no use. I was carrying a painful secret and had convinced myself that even my closest friends wouldn't understand.

What was my secret? I was afraid I would be rejected.

Three months prior, my fiancé had broken our engagement after becoming attracted to another young woman at school. I'd endured the humiliation of a public breakup. I'd suffered the pain of a broken heart. In the process, I'd compared myself to the other woman and become convinced that I must be ugly and sorely lacking in talent and social graces. *Obviously that's true, or he wouldn't have dumped me,* I reasoned.

Rather than admitting my fear of rejection and acknowledging its destructive force, I allowed it to paralyze me. *Who would want to be with me for a whole weekend? No one. I'll just stay behind and make it easy for everyone.* As my friends drove away to celebrate the best weekend of the year, I crawled between sterile sheets, desperately wishing for freedom from the chains that held me captive but afraid to confide in anyone lest doing so invite further rejection.

Twenty-five years passed before I mustered the courage to tell other women that I feared rejection. And guess what happened when I did? No one laughed. They listened quietly and nodded their heads in empathy. Some later drew me aside and whispered their own stories. That's when I began to realize how many others struggle with the same fear and how deep it runs.

Fear of Rejection Takes Root

Our front yard reminds me of a mini-orchard. A peach tree leans against our house near our bedroom window. (We pick peaches for breakfast simply by reaching out the window!) Two apple trees, a plum tree, loganberry bushes, and raspberry plants hang heavy with fruit each summer. They thrive with little effort on our part, thank goodness, because neither Gene nor I pretend to be gardeners. We prune a little here, lop off a branch there, and hope the rain and sunshine do their job at the right time.

I'm not a pro among green thumbers, but I can usually recognize an agricultural intruder when I see one. This morning, as I filled a bucket with raspberries, I discovered morning glory vines wound around the plants. Insidious horticultural creatures, they are. Oh yes, the white flowers look pretty, but the vines are another story. They creep and twist and tangle, threatening to choke the life from the healthy plants they hug. If left unchecked in our climate, these vines stake their turf and take over the territory. Once they've taken root, they're nearly impossible to get rid of.

Morning glory vines remind me of the fear of rejection. It too takes over the territory if left unchecked. I hate to admit it, but I'm an expert in *this* field. I'd love to stand before you and say, "I've conquered this fear," but I'd be lying if I did.

I'm finding this a difficult chapter to write. As I've researched, remembered, outlined, and prayed, the Holy Spirit has shown me that the fear of rejection took root in my childhood and still has its tendrils wound around my heart. But for some unknown reason, I hadn't identified its lingering presence in my life as easily as I spotted the morning glory vines amid the raspberries.

I can recall a truckload of not-so-nice memories that have contributed to my fear of rejection. For instance, I remember the feeling of dread in my stomach each time the PE teacher divided the class into two groups and appointed two captains. I watched and waited in agony as those captains chose the players they wanted for their teams. Inevitably, they picked their best friends and the strongest athletes first. One by one, the line of hopefuls dwindled. *Pick me, pick me,* I wished in silence, but my wish was never granted. I may as well have been wearing a flashing neon sign: REJECT! REJECT! REJECT!

Then came the girlie cliques at school. Membership excluded those whose clothes weren't the right style or color, those whose grades were either too high or too low, those whose parents were considered too strict or too poor, those who for whatever reason failed to meet someone's made-up standard. I did have friends, but I never broke into the cool group. That carried a feeling of rejection, but it was nothing compared to what other girls, especially Alice, must have felt.

Alice was the girl who sat behind me in fifth grade. She lived across the tracks in the neighborhood where "the poor people" lived. Most of the fifth-grade girls wore pants to school, but Alice wore cotton dresses that looked as if they'd been pulled from a dumpster. Her hair needed a good shampoo and brushing. Her shoes were two sizes too big, and her jacket was three sizes too small. Worse yet for Alice, she was born with a cleft palate, and there was no talk of surgical repair. When recess came, she stayed indoors and buried herself in library books. Today, from an adult's perspective, I suspect her heart was breaking. Reading was likely her defense mechanism to protect herself from rejection on the playground.

Seeds of rejection are often planted in our homes as well. Perhaps your memories have few hugs and even less positive affirmation. Maybe Mom or Dad peppered their conversation with comments like these:

> "Why can't your grades be as good as your sister's?"
>
> "Your siblings never cause us grief. What's wrong with *you?*"
>
> "I can hardly wait until you leave home."
>
> "Life was so easy before you came along."

Maybe they brushed off your requests for attention: "Later. I'm too busy now." But later never came.

The movie *Walk the Line* graphically portrays a parent's rejection of his child. In one scene, the eldest of two preteen brothers dies tragically. Rather than scooping the younger brother into his arms and grieving with him, the drunken father yells, "The devil took the wrong son!" Oh, the pain!

Perhaps you were abused by someone who should have protected you. "Don't you dare tell anyone," he threatened. "If you do, I won't love you anymore. And besides, no one will believe you. They'll just laugh at you." That person's mentality was warped, but you didn't know that. You were just a terrified little girl who desperately wanted to feel cherished and safe, so you obeyed for fear of rejection and abandonment.

Our specifics are different, but most of us have experienced verbal or nonverbal rejection at one time or another. The seed was planted and took root in our little-girl hearts. And because we've never identified and dealt with it, it remains twisted and tangled through our minds and emotions today. Now we're big girls. Years have passed, but the fear of rejection has not.

What's the Big Deal About Big-Girl Fears?

The fear of rejection impacts our lives in several ways. Consider, for example, the physical effects. Many folks experience these when asked to speak before an audience. Our hearts pound, our stomachs feel queasy or tie themselves in a knot, our mouths go bone-dry, our hands and knees shake. Sometimes our voices quiver. Physical jitters are a nervous reaction caused by fear—the fear of rejection.

Every summer, our ministry hosts three family camps to which we invite various speakers to teach from God's Word. Last week, the speaker was a 28-year-old pastor who attended our camp as a teenager. Now he stood as God's messenger before the staff and 120 strangers, and the poor fellow looked a tad scared. He shuffled his notes and then said, "Before I begin, I need to pray. You see, I'm *really* nervous. This is the first time I've taught at a family camp, and frankly, I want you to like me."

Bingo! I loved his honesty. His words "I want you to like me" acknowledged the reality of the fear of rejection. I also appreciated the words that followed: "But this isn't about me. It's about what God wants to say to you this week." Despite his desire for acceptance, the pastor recognized his responsibility to speak truth rather than tickle the listeners' ears.

Some women camouflage their fear of rejection by wearing a mask of artificiality. Sadly enough, this happens way too often within Christian circles. Here's a fictitious example: Suzie Smiley has been married for 12 years to a man who resembles Jekyll and Hyde. In the confines of their home, he's verbally and physically abusive toward her and the kids. He's also addicted to pornography. Suzie's fed up with his Internet antics, and she's downright scared for her family's safety. But no one outside their home suspects anything evil in her husband's character. In fact, he's a deacon in their church.

Sunday after Sunday, Suzie greets her Christian friends with empty platitudes. "How are you today?" she asks. "Fine," they say. "And yourself?"

"Fine, just fine."

On the outside, Suzy wears a plastic smile. Inside, she's desperately longing for help, but she's afraid of what people will think of her, her husband, and their Christian testimony if she admits what's going on behind closed doors. And so she maintains their cover. Rather than risk rejection, she hides behind a mask of artificiality and pretends that everything is fine.

Perhaps you've done something similar. I have. When our kids were preschoolers, I had days when I felt stressed to the max. I'd be hollering at someone for something when, sure enough, the phone would ring and interrupt my tirade. It's amazing how a ringing phone affects one's vocal chords.

"Hello," I'd say, sweet as cotton candy. The person on the other end was never the wiser—unless my windows were open and she lived next door.

If I could relive those years, I'd do a few things differently. For one, I'd admit when I needed a break *before* the breaking point came and my kids took the brunt. Why didn't I do that then? Because I was afraid that my image as a perfect mother might be tarnished if others knew I felt overwhelmed. I believed a lie and allowed the fear of rejection to hold me captive.

The mask of artificiality fits any woman bearing a secret shame. In 1996, approximately 246,600 American evangelical women aborted their babies.[1] On the outside, when these gals sit in our church pews, everything appears hunky-dory. But the inside scene… well, that's usually another story. Shame is often slowly devouring these precious women, but many are afraid to seek help and healing lest others reject them for what they've done.

A.W. Tozer says that humans share a desire to "put the best foot forward and hide from the world our real inward poverty." He says, "There is hardly a man or woman who dares to be just what he or she is without doctoring up the impression. The fear of being found out gnaws like rodents within their hearts."[2]

Our longing for leaving good impressions and being accepted by others also impacts our relationships with those around us. When my fiancé rejected me, I convinced myself that I was ugly and worthless. As a result, I found it difficult to believe that anyone else would think otherwise. Rather than risk being hurt again, I withdrew from girlfriends who would have wrapped their arms around me and offered loving support. And it didn't stop there.

I wore my mask of artificiality well for several years. During that time, I met and married Gene. He treated me like a princess. At least once a day he told me he loved me. But my ongoing fear of rejection caused me to harbor nagging doubts.

Oh yeah? Well, I've heard "I love you" before, but those words didn't mean much then. How do I know I can trust you?

I never spoke those words aloud, but my mind entertained them. I also wrestled with jealousy. Gene never gave me reason to doubt his integrity, but my fear of rejection left me feeling threatened whenever he spoke with another woman. Ten years passed before I removed my mask and admitted my fears to Gene. Doing so finally freed me to enter wholeheartedly into my marriage. Until then I hadn't truly loved my husband as he deserved. I'd withheld a part of my heart from him, hiding it in a safe place in case he left me.

When I conducted my fear survey, numerous participants said they struggle with issues related to premarital sex. Memories haunt them. Lust tempts them. Inappropriate mental images seem permanently embedded in their minds. These women long for freedom from the past, but they refuse to seek counsel or share their struggle. And why not? You guessed it. They're afraid that others will reject them if they admit failure in that area of their lives. And so they go on, halfheartedly engaged with their spouses yet craving greater intimacy in marriage.

Maladaptive behavior is another by-product of the fear of rejection. For instance, we lie to conceal our less-than-perfect personality and performance. Marilyn Meberg writes this in *The Zippered Heart:*

> Most of the lies we tell are motivated by the fear that the truth would not put us in a good light. We lie to prevent others from seeing or knowing the truth about us—a truth that exposes us as less than perfect. We are ashamed of being less than perfect; we think the lie preserves our image. Similarly, when we present a false identity, we hope our mask will cause us to appear more acceptable, winsome, capable, worthy of praise, and lovable. Because shame messages convince us we are not lovable or capable, maybe a false ID will make up for the inherently inadequate person we perceive ourselves to be.[3]

Have you ever tried to conceal a mistake at work to protect your image? Have you ever exaggerated a story to impress others? Have you ever gossiped about another woman to make yourself look better than her? Then you can identify.

Sometimes the fear of rejection causes us to manipulate others so we can maintain control and thereby prove our worth. Or we drink excessively to deaden the memories of past rejections and ease the blow of possible present rejections. Or we engage in wrongful sexual behavior in our attempts to find acceptance and love.

I wonder if Satan throws a hellish party each time he dupes one of God's daughters into believing his lies. *You're not worth much,* he hisses. *No one loves you. And they'd love you even less if they knew the truth about you.* He cackles and snorts and snivels, and then he slaps his shackles on our hearts.

Perhaps you're peering into the entrance of a scary-looking cave labeled Fear of Rejection. The treasure you seek—freedom—lies within its dark confines.

You crave freedom. You want respite from the pain. You want to throw away your mask of artificiality, to run and laugh and twirl and dance like no one's watching, but an inner voice restrains you: *Don't do it. What will people think if they knew the real you?*

Don't heed that voice! Take the first step. Face the fear of rejection. Enter the cave where healing begins, my dear sister, for until you do, you will never find the treasure you seek.

Beth's Story

Beth and I met several years ago when she attended a mother-daughter retreat at our camp. We bonded immediately and agreed to stay in touch. Several years passed, during which time we visited two or three times. But one day a letter I'd mailed was returned with a message stamped on the envelope: "Moved. No forwarding address."

That's odd, I thought. *Where did she go? Why didn't she send her new address?* I felt as though she'd dropped off the earth and fallen from my orbit. I had no way of knowing that she was in extreme pain.

Beth recently reentered my life through a series of God-ordained circumstances and told me her story. She'd grown up in a home that outsiders considered ideal. In reality, however, her father sexually and physically abused her for at least ten years. He threatened,

"If you don't cooperate with me, or if you tell Mom, she'll leave." Her mother, on the other hand, never touched her, never cuddled her, and never said "I love you." Nothing Beth did for her was good enough. Even though the relationship was already strained, the threat of absolute abandonment terrified her, so she maintained silence.

Beth prayed to receive Christ as her Savior while attending summer camp as an eight-year-old. She was baptized at age 14, and that's when she told her dad, "Don't touch me again. I belong to Jesus." She worked hard and saved money for college, anticipating the day when she could move from home. She married at age 21 and raised four children.

On the exterior, things appeared pretty good. But the interior— Beth's heart—was a disaster. *I'm unlovable. I must be an awful person or my parents wouldn't have treated me as they did. I dare not let others know my shortcomings or they'll hate me too.* Perfectionism drove her activities as she sought others' approval. She tried to control her circumstances so she could look good in their eyes. When control eluded her, she lashed out in anger.

At age 34, afraid that she might physically hurt her children the same way her dad, in angry fits, had harmed her, Beth faced her fear of rejection and chose to seek professional help. First, she mustered the courage to tell her church secretary and pastor about her abusive past. To her relief, they didn't push her away. Instead, they offered counseling and prayer. Next, she shared her story with coworkers at the Christian school where she was employed. They too embraced her and began praying for her regularly.

Almost a year later, Beth discovered that her siblings had also suffered abuse. When her parents announced that they were coming for a two-week visit and planned to stay in her home, she knew she must protect her own children from possible harm.

With her husband, her pastor, and the church secretary by her side, Beth read a loving letter of confrontation to her dad about what he'd done. She urged him to seek counseling for sexual addiction.

This time, her fear came true. Her mother and father left in a huff and refused all contact for the next five years.

Her parents' abandonment reinforced Beth's fear of rejection. *I was right. I AM an ugly person.* Once again she retreated behind her mask and stayed there until her mid-forties, seeking to please people and prove her perfection through performance while condemning herself as a hypocrite.

Finally, total despair gripped her. She dropped out of women's ministries and Sunday school. She ended her involvement on the church worship team and missions committee. And she cried to God, *I don't want to live any longer without the sense of being real!*

God heard and answered His daughter's desperate cry. A short time later, Beth met a pastor named Sharon. The two women bonded. Sharon too had suffered sexual abuse in her childhood. She could relate to Beth's self-hatred and fear of rejection, but she knew the joy of freedom. Bit by bit, Beth removed her mask of artificiality, and Sharon poured God's love into her life through listening, praying, and directing her to the truth of His Word.

One afternoon Beth decided to swing by Sharon's church. As she approached, she heard a delighted squeal from inside the building— Sharon had looked out a window and seen her coming. The pastor burst through the door and dashed down the sidewalk toward her. She threw her arms around Beth and gave her a huge hug.

That simple moment, says Beth, marked the turning point in her life: "I felt like the prodigal child being welcomed by the father. I realized that this friendship wasn't just about Sharon and me. In reality, it was a picture of God's love for me." She says that moment would never have happened if she hadn't entered the cave she feared and faced the risk of rejection by seeking help to move forward.

Understanding God's unconditional love for her has freed Beth from the chains of perfectionism—she knows that God loves her for who she is, not for how she performs. She enjoys an open and real relationship with her husband and kids. She admits that she still wrestles with self-rejection, but at least now she recognizes its source and refutes it with God's truth. And therein lies the ultimate key to freedom.[4]

The Ultimate Key to Freedom

The ultimate key to freedom from the fear of rejection is found woven like a scarlet thread through every page of Christian Scripture. Story upon story shows God's unconditional love for messed-up mankind. Every account reveals His hand extended to the sinful, the broken, the hopeless, and the outcasts. Each tale illustrates His grace freely given to less-than-perfect mortals who humble themselves before Him. Isn't that amazing?

We have a difficult time wrapping our minds around such love in action. It supersedes our wildest imagination. It's like nothing we know. And that's probably why we struggle with the fear of rejection. We simply can't understand how a perfect God stoops to love imperfect people.

We've been culturally programmed to think perfection is the key to acceptance: Top achievers get the promotions. The most beautiful women win the pageants. The strongest win the race. In reality, the key to acceptance in God's eyes is admitting our imperfection. In His famous Sermon on the Mount, Jesus said, "God blesses those who realize their need for him, for the Kingdom of Heaven is given to them" (Matthew 5:3). His words contradict what society teaches.

Society says we're to be independent, intelligent, beautiful, and brave—or at least make others believe we are. Admitting otherwise only causes others to lose respect for us, question our worth, or—heaven forbid—reject us.

But God's truth says otherwise. He embraces those who admit weakness and cry to Him for help. He loves us not because *we're* so good, but because *He's* so good. He loves us not for what we *should* be but for who we *are,* complete with emotional scars, spiritual warts, and physical stretch marks.

Brennan Manning describes God's love for us in these words:

"God loves you in the morning sun and the evening rain, without caution or regret. If God ceased to be love, God would cease to be God."[5]

The Bible is filled with stories that show God's love for people whom others rejected. Do you remember Zacchaeus—the vertically challenged money mongrel? Religious leaders looked the other way when they saw him coming, but Jesus invited Himself to his home for dinner (Luke 19:2-10).

And there's the woman at Jacob's well. She had three strikes against her—she was a female, she was a Samaritan, and she was promiscuous. Her status in that culture forced her to draw water from the well when no one else was around. But one day Jesus showed up and offered her living water (John 4:5-26).

How about Joseph? His own brothers threw him down a well and later sold him into slavery. Then the poor guy landed in prison after being falsely accused of rape by his boss' wife when he refused to sleep with her. People rejected Joseph, but God didn't. Instead, He exalted him to a key position of authority in the land (Genesis 37:23-28; 39:7-20; 41:41).

Let's not forget Hagar (Genesis 16:1-13; 21:8-20). She was an Egyptian, a foreigner in the culture in which she lived. She was also a servant, considered a piece of property owned by her mistress and compelled to do whatever her mistress wished. So when her barren boss, Sarai, decided to present her husband, Abram, with a child, Hagar was forced to sleep with him. Any children born from that union would belong to Sarai, and that would make her look like a good wife.

The scheme might have worked had Hagar not displayed an "I'm better than you are" attitude toward her mistress when the pregnancy test showed positive. Her attitude annoyed Sarai, who retaliated by treating Hagar so harshly that she decided to run away (Genesis 16:6).

I wonder what thoughts ran through Hagar's head as she sat destitute in the wilderness. I doubt they were happy thoughts. Perhaps they went something like this: *Serves you right. You're just a lousy servant girl anyway. Now you've run away, so you must be a coward too. You'll die out here, and no one will even miss you.*

But God loved Hagar. Despite her character flaws, He stooped to speak with her in the desert. "Go back to Sarai," He said. "You'll have a son. Name him Ishmael, for I've heard about your misery."

That must have been *some* encounter—Scripture says thereafter Hagar referred to the Lord as "the God who sees me" (verse 13). Sarai had rejected her, but she knew the Lord hadn't. Perhaps that knowledge carried her through the next 17 years. After all, it couldn't have been easy working for a jealous employer. Toss PMS into the mix, and look out!

But the day came when Hagar faced another blow. It happened when 17-year-old Ishmael taunted toddler Isaac, the miracle child of Sarai (now called *Sarah*). It doesn't take a rocket scientist to know that wasn't a smart thing to do, considering the tension between Hagar and Sarah. When Sarah saw what was happening, she yelled at Abram (now called *Abraham*) to get rid of "that servant" and her son. She wouldn't let Hagar's name cross her lips. And she seemed to forget that Ishmael was her responsibility. Scripture tells what happened next:

> So Abraham got up early the next morning, prepared food for the journey, and strapped a container of water to Hagar's shoulders. He sent her away with their son, and she walked out into the wilderness of Beersheba, wandering aimlessly. When the water was gone, she left the boy in the shade of a bush. Then she went and sat down by herself about a hundred yards away. "I don't want to watch the boy die," she said, as she burst into tears (Genesis 21:14-16).

Use your sanctified imagination. Can you see Hagar squatting on the sun-baked soil, the blazing sun beating on her head? She buries her face in her dusty shawl and cries bitter tears as she thinks of her

QUOTABLE QUOTES

Consider these thoughts as you seek to move beyond your fear of rejection:

1. Acknowledge that, as God's daughters, we're engaged in a spiritual battle for our souls. Beware of Satan's weapon called self-rejection!

   I have come to realize that the greatest trap in our life is not success, popularity or power, but self-rejection…I am constantly surprised at how quickly I give in to this temptation. As soon as someone accuses me or criticizes me, I am rejected, left alone or abandoned, I find myself thinking: "Well that proves once again that I am a nobody." Instead of taking a critical look at the circumstances or trying to understand my own and others' limitations, I tend to blame myself—not just for what I did, but for who I am. My dark side says: "I am no good…I deserve to be pushed aside, forgotten, rejected and abandoned."[6]

   HENRI NOUWEN

2. Reprogram your brain by agreeing with God to love yourself unconditionally.

   Many of us feel we can perhaps love ourselves if we do something well, if our performance is good. Maybe then we deserve being loved. But how can we love ourselves when we make mistakes and do embarrassing things? That's the whole point…If we love ourselves unconditionally, then even when we blow it badly, making huge or small mistakes, we do not waver in our agreement with God that we are still loveable—because He says we are![7]

   MARILYN MEBERG

3. Open up to others regarding your weaknesses and failures.

   I am not a spiritual giant. I am a poor, weak, sinful man with hereditary faults and limited talents, loved unconditionally as I am, not as I should be. When I can let that be known in some way, there is less to hide, and I am less tempted to offer you the bright, shining image of my impostor self. This "imposter" me feels I have to build up an illusion of perfection in order to be loved.[8]

   BRENNAN MANNING

dehydrated teenager laying about 300 feet away—close enough so he knows she's there, but far enough away so she can't see him take his last breath. Then the lies start rolling in: *God doesn't really see us. We're going to die. No one cares. No one wants us.*

But God once again rushes to Hagar's rescue. Unlike Sarah, who called her merely "that servant," God calls this distraught woman by name: "Hagar, what's wrong?" He consoles her and gives her direction: "Do not be afraid! Go comfort your boy, for I'm going to make a great nation from his descendants." And then He demonstrates His love for her again by opening her eyes to see a well of water nearby.

Zacchaeus wasn't perfect. Neither was the Samaritan woman, or Joseph, or Hagar. Neither are you and I. But that doesn't matter to God, who loves us not because *we're* so good, but because *He's* so good.

People rejected our Bible-time friends, but God loved them, comforted them, and encouraged them. The same is true for us today. People will reject us for one reason or another, and that hurts. But God's love for us never fails.

Do you believe that? Do you know in your heart that He will never turn you away? If so, I rejoice with you. If not, pause for a moment before reading any further. Ask the Lord to show you what is hindering you from understanding and accepting His love for you. Then ask Him to remove all hindrances and flood your mind with the truth that will set you free from the fear of rejection. When you pray a prayer like that and believe He'll answer, you can rest assured He will!

What's Love Got to Do with It?

Several years ago, a popular song asked the question, "What's love got to do with it?" In overcoming the fear of rejection, the answer is, "Everything!"

Babies are born into this world with a need to be loved. Those who aren't held and played with fail to thrive, as seen in over-crowded, understaffed orphanages in poverty-stricken countries.

That innate longing for love stays with us for life. We want to be cherished, embraced, and treasured. But we live in a fallen world, so that doesn't always happen. How can we survive if our needs go unmet or are trampled underfoot by someone we love?

You met Wanda in a previous chapter. She spoke about the lessons she'd learned in the storm, about being married to a man whose drug addiction created havoc in their home and eventually led to divorce.

Wanda entered that marriage as a 19-year-old woman, head-over-heels in love, clueless that Roger was heavily addicted to cocaine. It didn't take long to find out. Sometimes Roger would leave for work on Friday morning and not return until Sunday night or Monday. He broke promises. He skipped birthday parties, anniversaries, Christmas dinners, children's concerts, and award ceremonies.

During those years, Wanda spent sleepless nights wondering where her husband was, waiting and listening for the door to open. She answered countless phone calls from the police and the hospital. She made numerous visits to the penitentiary when he served jail time. She sought counseling, visited treatment centers, and read self-help books. Nothing removed the knot in her stomach as she fought to maintain normalcy for her family. And always she wondered, *Am I not enough for him? Why has he chosen his friends and cocaine over his family? Is life too dull with us?*

Several years into the tumult, Wanda joined a church where she attended women's meetings. She read an occasional devotional if she could drag herself from bed before the kids woke, and she prayed when she felt like it. But when Roger faced a conviction that carried a possible five-year sentence, Wanda broke. She sensed God telling her to get serious about her relationship with Him. She was raising two kids alone and working full-time, but she rose at

4:30 a.m. to pray and read God's Word. And as she did, she began understanding the depth of His love for her.

"Through those years, Jesus truly became my husband," says Wanda. "He became my strength and comfort, my counselor, and my best friend. We developed a relationship that has no *have-tos* about spending time together. It's all about *get-tos*. I have the privilege of spending time with the Creator of the universe every day, the One who knows me more intimately than anyone else does and yet loves me with an everlasting love."

Wanda refers to Ephesians 3:19 as a favorite verse: "May you experience the love of Christ, though it is so great you will never fully understand it. Then you will be filled with the fullness of life and power that comes from God."

"Knowing God's love for us far outweighs any treasure we could possibly pursue or possess," Wanda says. "Nothing else will ever satisfy us, and no rejection, no matter how severe, will ever take it away."[9]

What's love—God's love—got to do with it? Everything!

Beth Moore says, "The fear or the feeling of being unloved is probably our greatest source of insecurity, whether or not we can always articulate it."[10] Referring to Proverbs 19:22 (NIV)—"What a man desires is unfailing love"—she says that the word *desires* implies a deep craving. Each of us craves an undying, unalterable, unconditional love, but we'll never find it in a human being. Beth says that God's Word uses the phrase "unfailing love" 32 times, and each instance refers to God Himself. God created us with a void that only He can fill. Only He can meet our deepest need. And when we invite Him to do so, He quiets our fear of rejection.

Back to Wanda's story for a moment. Before she began spending deliberate time with the Lord, she lived each day with a broken heart, not knowing how she could continue to exist. But immersing herself in the Word changed that. She filled her emotional cup with truth about God's love for her, and that knowledge transformed her perspective.

Beth Moore says we all have unmet needs. We carry them around like an empty cup, expecting others to fill it.

> Whether we seek to have our cup filled through approval, affirmation, control, success, or immediate gratification, we are miserable until something is in it. I have come to dearly love and appreciate Psalm 143:8 [NIV]: "Let the morning bring me word of your unfailing love, for I have put my trust in you. Show me the way I should go, for to you I lift up my soul." What a heavy yoke is shattered when we awaken in the morning, bring our hearts, minds, and souls and all their "needs" to the Great Soulologist, offer Him our empty cups, and ask Him to fill them with Himself! No one is more pleasurable to be around than a person who has had her cup filled by the Lord Jesus Christ. He is the only One who is never overwhelmed by the depth and length of our need.[11]

So long as we're warm and breathing, we face the possibility of rejection, and with it comes disappointment and pain. How can we survive? By following Wanda's example and Beth's advice and filling our cup with God. He alone, in His unfailing love, can meet our craving for love and acceptance.

✦ POINTS FOR PROGRESS ✦

1. Read 1 Peter 2:4: "Come to Christ, who is the living cornerstone of God's temple. He was rejected by the people, but he is precious to God who chose him."

   - Why did the people reject Christ?
   - What did that rejection look like in His life?
   - How did He respond to those who rejected Him?
   - What does that teach us about our response toward those who reject us?

2. Galatians 2:20 says, "I myself no longer live, but Christ lives in me. So I live my life in this earthly body by trusting in the Son of God, who loved me and gave himself for me." What truths in this verse refute an attitude of self-rejection?

3. Scripture tells us to love our neighbors as ourselves. How does self-rejection hinder us from loving others as God commands?

4. Beth Moore stresses the importance of inviting God to fill up our empty cup every morning. On a scale of one to ten with ten being filled to the brim with God, how would you rate the state of your cup? If it's lacking, what changes do you need to make?

5. Wanda says that the hymn "The Solid Rock" sustained her during her struggle with rejection. Read the lyrics and tell what phrases encourage you and why.

THE SOLID ROCK
WILLIAM B. BRADBURY

My hope is built on nothing less
Than Jesus' blood and righteousness;
I dare not trust the sweetest frame,
But wholly lean on Jesus' name.

When darkness veils His lovely face,
I rest on His unchanging grace;
In every high and stormy gale,
My anchor holds within the veil.

His oath, His covenant, His blood,
Support me in the whelming flood;
When all around my soul gives way,
He then is all my hope and stay.

When He shall come with trumpet sounds,
Oh, may I then in Him be found;
Dressed in His righteousness alone,
Faultless to stand before the throne.

On Christ the solid Rock, I stand;
All other ground is sinking sand;
All other ground is sinking sand.

✦ PROMISES TO PONDER ✦

O God, you are my God;
   I earnestly search for you.
My soul thirsts for you;
   my whole body longs for you
in this parched and weary land
   where there is no water...
Your unfailing love is better to me than life itself;
   how I praise you!...
You satisfy me more than the richest of foods.
   I will praise you with songs of joy (Psalm 63:1,3,5).

So many enemies against one man—
   all of them trying to kill me.
To them I'm just a broken-down wall
   or a tottering fence.
They plan to topple me from my high position.
   They delight in telling lies about me.
They are friendly to my face,
   but they curse me in their hearts.
I wait quietly before God,
   for my hope is in him.
He alone is my rock and my salvation,
   my fortress where I will not be shaken.
My salvation and my honor come from God alone.

He is my refuge, a rock where no enemy can reach me…
Power, O God, belongs to you;
   unfailing love, O Lord, is yours
(Psalm 62:3-7,11-12).

O God, insolent people rise up against me;
   violent people are trying to kill me.
   And you mean nothing to them.
But you, O Lord, are a merciful and gracious God,
   slow to get angry,
   full of unfailing love and truth.
Look down and have mercy on me.
   Give strength to your servant;
   yes, save me, for I am your servant.
Send me a sign of your favor.
   Then those who hate me will be put to shame,
   for you, O LORD, help and comfort me
(Psalm 86:14-17).

✦ PRAYING THE PROMISES ✦

Dear Father, my soul thirsts for You, and my entire body longs for You. Nothing, not even the sweetest human relationship, satisfies me like You do. Your unfailing love is better than life itself. I praise You, for You alone are worthy, faithful One. Amen.

Dear God, sometimes I feel as though enemies surround me. Even my friends have turned on me and are saying hurtful things about me behind my back. But I wait on You. You are my rock and my salvation. I hide in You as my fortress. No one who rejects me can touch me there. Thank You for loving me and for keeping me with Your power and unfailing love. Amen.

Dear Father, someone who doesn't know You has rejected me and is trying to harm my reputation. Please, Lord, have mercy on me in this situation. Give me strength. Show me Your favor. Comfort me, Father. Shower me with Your unfailing love, for then she will be ashamed of what she's done. Amen.

Saying Goodbye *to the* Ghosts *in* My Past

*Fear is that little darkroom where
negatives are developed.*

Michael Pritchard

Jana Lapel's future sparkled like a billion-dollar diamond—or so it appeared to outsiders. A Shirley Temple look-alike, she launched her public singing career at age three when she sang "Jesus Loves Me" to her family's church congregation. Ten years later she was performing on television. And three years after that, she hosted her own radio program. No one suspected that behind her blonde curls and beaming smile lay a broken heart.

For 17 years, Jana endured sexual abuse by her uncle—a Sunday school teacher and youth group leader. She couldn't understand what was happening to her, nor did she wish to hurt her family by talking about it, so she hid her secret and began a quest for true love.

Jana's search lasted for more than two decades and resulted in four divorces. She wrestled with a long list of emotional and mental difficulties—nervous breakdowns, panic attacks, depression, anxiety, and psychosomatic physical ailments. Although she was somehow able to launch a professional singing and acting career during that time, shame and self-blame haunted her like an unrelenting specter. She felt far from God, praying only when she felt afraid on a turbulent flight or when her son was sick. *After all,* she reasoned, *God doesn't care about me anymore. I'm too far gone for Him.*

That misperception consumed her. On one occasion, a woman invited her to attend a luncheon at which Dale Evans Rogers was scheduled to speak. Jana hesitated—she felt unworthy of spending time in the presence of Christian women whose lives seemed in order. But the thought of seeing and hearing someone else in show business prompted her to accept the invitation.

During the program, Dale shared her testimony and then instructed the guests to close their eyes and bow their heads. She said, "If you need the Lord like I've needed the Lord, raise your hand. Let me know that you've said yes to Jesus."

Rather than raise her hand, Jana raised her index finger under the white tablecloth. *I know You don't want to associate with me, God, but do You see my finger?* she asked. *I'm trying to tell You that I need You, but I'm so ashamed of myself. I'm so far gone—probably too far for You to help me.*[1]

Despite Jana's feelings, nothing could have been further from the truth.

Beauty for Ashes

I'll continue Jana's story in a minute. But for a moment, stop and ponder this fact: Everyone on this earth has a past. And that past plays itself through our minds like a video stuck on permanent replay. Some scenes recall treasured memories. Others replay situations that have left us feeling resentful or hurt, angry or disillusioned.

Perhaps your circumstances are similar to Jana's—you've endured immense pain at another person's hands. Maybe you were raped, robbed, or ridiculed. Perhaps a coworker damaged your reputation by spreading rumors at the office, or someone swindled you financially.

Hiding what happened or harboring bitterness toward the offender has only compounded your grief.

On the other hand, maybe you made a bad choice in the past and the memories linger. You lied on your résumé to land a job you really wanted. You yelled false accusations at your husband or smacked your children in a moment of rage. You became emotionally involved with a guy at work or on the Internet and…well, one thing led to another. And now regret has taken up permanent residence.

Maybe your past is filled with trauma or grief or disappointment. You witnessed a crime or an accident or lost a loved one in a tragedy. You gave up a baby for adoption, had an abortion, suffered a miscarriage, or lost a child. You felt the sting of a lover's rejection, or you stung someone else. You suffered the angst and embarrassment of bankruptcy or were overlooked when the boss handed out a coveted promotion.

The list of possibilities seems endless. Whatever your past circumstances, they may be hurting you today. Fear is holding you back from becoming the woman you were meant to be—the fear of being found out, the fear of facing painful consequences, the fear of repeating history or of making the necessary changes to avoid repeating history. So you're stuck—unable to move into a bright future and unable to leave the past behind. And you wonder, *Can I possibly say goodbye and good riddance to the ghosts in my past? Can I somehow experience true freedom?*

Yes, you can. I can say that with confidence because of who God is and what He promises to do for those whose hearts are wholly committed to following Him. I've seen it happen over and over again. As a freelance writer, I've interviewed dozens of people with stories of brokenness and have listened to them tell about how God has rebuilt their lives in ways they'd never imagined. I've read the Scriptures and seen His love transform those who felt all hope was gone. And I've experienced His healing touch in my own life.

Crossing moral boundaries in my teenage dating days left me feeling dirty and undesirable. When Gene proposed, I admitted my past failures to him. He hugged me, assured me of his forgiveness, and promised me that he would never hold them against me. He held true to his word, but my shame clung to me like a stubborn stain.

I felt like a hypocrite when I shopped for my wedding gown. The ghost of my past haunted me relentlessly: *You don't deserve to wear white on your wedding day,* it whispered over and over. I agreed and settled for a champagne-colored dress instead.

When other women commented on the color, I said I chose it because it suited me better than stark white. In my heart, however, I was doing penance. I wanted to experience pure, unadulterated joy as I planned for my wedding and anticipated married life, but the ghost haunted and taunted day in and day out. And it persisted for nearly a decade after my wedding. I went through the motions of everyday life and managed to do so successfully, but emotionally and spiritually I wasn't free to be the woman or wife God wanted me to be.

But God had better things in store for me than wallowing in my past. He had a purpose for my life and knew I wouldn't experience it if I insisted on staying in the muck and mire. He prompted me to read His Word on a regular basis, to make relationship with Him a priority over service for Him, and to develop the discipline of praising Him for who He is. It worked. The pain from my past dissipated, replaced by a joy I'd never thought possible. Yes, some scars remain, but scars don't hurt. They simply remind me that healing has taken place.

Reliving past failures or disappointments may leave us feeling as though we have nothing to offer. We've made lousy choices. We've royally messed up. Like Jana, we feel as though we've gone too far for God. But nothing's further from the truth. God Himself says so: "To all who mourn in Israel, he will give beauty for ashes, joy instead of mourning, praise instead of despair. For the LORD has planted them like strong and graceful oaks for his own glory" (Isaiah 61:3).

Notice the contrasts in that verse. Focusing on past failures leaves us with nothing but ashes, mourning, and despair. Sounds bleak, doesn't it? But when we admit what we've done and receive Christ's forgiveness, or face the pain of an offense committed against us and then give our pain to the Lord, He replaces its ugliness with beauty, joy, and praise. And because of His unfailing love and almighty power, He's able to use even our failures for our growth and His glory.

Jana's story proves this is true. Her life's downward spiral stopped when she attended a women's Bible study where she admitted her fear of God's refusal to forgive her past. The leader's response shocked her.

"You insult God when you say you're too bad for Him to save you!" she said. "He died on the cross for your sins, and you're refusing to accept His gift to you!"

Those words changed Jana's perspective. She realized that her limited understanding of God's character and work had hindered her from breaking free from her past. She wept and prayed, *Lord, I've spent my life running from You and looking for love in all the wrong places. I give You full control. I want to go where You want me to go.*

That's when the healing began. Her panic attacks decreased. She was able to forgive her uncle. Shame released its grip. She broke the silence and began talking honestly about her struggles. And God began using her for His own glory.

Today Jana uses her God-given acting and singing ability to minister to children. She paints her face, dons a red-and-white checked costume, and calls herself Christy Clown. She shares love, laughter, and life lessons with kids in school assemblies, at birthday parties, and at corporate events where employees bring their children.

Jana also tells her story to women's groups. Even the toughest prostitutes at inner-city missions wipe tears from their eyes as they listen to her message of hope and transformation. "God has turned all my bad stuff into something that can reach those who think they're too far gone for Him," she says.

Indeed He has. And He wants to do the same for you, my sister. Are you willing to trade yesterday's regrets and pain for today's joy and tomorrow's promise? The choice is yours. The glory is His.

Shed the Excess Weight

Last winter I spoke at a one-day women's conference in Saskatchewan, Canada. Temperatures plunged overnight, and fresh snow blanketed lawns and roadways on the morning of my flight home.

Several minutes after I'd settled into my airplane seat, the pilot made an announcement. "Well, folks, our takeoff will be delayed by a half hour or so," he said. "It appears that our plane turned into a popsicle overnight. The maintenance fellows will deice the wings, and we'll be underway shortly. Thanks for your patience."

The Rocky Mountains stand like sky-high armored soldiers between Saskatchewan and my home in British Columbia. *A half-hour delay? No problem. Take as much time as you need. Removing the excess weight to fly over those mountains safely sounds like a good idea to me!*

As I waited, I thought about other forms of excess weight. I'd enjoyed a doughnut and coffee for breakfast, but that's not the kind of weight I mean! I was pondering issues that keep us grounded spiritually, encumbrances that hinder us from soaring to heavenly heights where we experience God on a regular and dynamic basis. Baggage from our past is one of those weights. We all carry it, although the content and size varies. While some have learned to deal with it and move on, many refuse to release it, even despite another's offer to help.

Imagine this for a moment—a middle-aged woman drags a boxcar-sized trunk behind her everywhere she goes. It contains memories of a lover's rejection, a friend's betrayal, a career disappointment, a critical remark, and more. The woman's load stresses her to the max. Day after day she puffs and pants and perspires.

"Let me take your trunk," offers a friend. He extends his hand and waits for her response.

She casts him an annoyed glance. "No thanks," she says. "I don't need your help. I can handle it." And off she goes again, puffing and panting and perspiring.

We look at this woman and think she's lost her mental marbles. As silly as it sounds, however, we do the same thing by insisting on lugging our baggage from the past—especially when a friend named Jesus stands by and offers to carry our load.

> Then Jesus said, "Come to me, all of you who are weary and carry heavy burdens, and I will give you rest. Take my yoke upon you. Let me teach you, because I am humble and gentle, and you will find rest for your souls. For my yoke fits perfectly, and the burden I give you is light" (Matthew 11:28-30).

Jesus never intended for us to carry the burden of a painful past. He knows its effect on us. It defeats us and keeps us grounded—unable to soar freely and experience the power-filled lives He wants for His daughters. And so He invites us to come to Him and pour out our hearts to Him as intimate friends, to draw on His supernatural strength and wisdom and power to see us through. When we do, we find healing rest.

The Greek word for *rest* means intermission, recreation, refreshment. What could be sweeter than a dose of heavenly refreshment for the weary? Imagine a spiritual version of a back massage or a hot tub soak for aching muscles! Doesn't that sound better than breaking our backs over burdens we don't have to carry?

This verse contains another truth worth noting. Jesus' invitation does *not* say, "Come to me, all ye perfect people with no baggage. Come to me, all of you who have never sinned. Come, all of you with pristine pasts."

Instead, His words are directed to men and women who have been hurt by people or circumstances, or who have been messed up by their own choices. Perhaps, like Jana, they're even afraid of asking God for help because they feel they've disappointed Him or gone beyond the reaches of His grace. These are the ones to whom Jesus offers His hand and says, "Come to me, and I will give you rest." And in His eyes, no one is beyond redemption.

The offer has been extended. There's no need to stagger under the weight of our past. God intends better things for us. We only need to say yes.

Ban the Backward Glance

Our pastor recently commented on a cartoon he'd seen. In the cartoon, one character counseled her friend by saying, "Life is like a cruise ship. Some people open their deck chairs on the back. When they sit there, they see only where they've been. Others open their chairs on the front. They look ahead and see where they're going." The counselee listened and said, "That sounds great, but I can't even figure out how to *open* my chair!"

This word picture contains wisdom relevant to each of us, regardless of our circumstances. Life consists of choices, and we're responsible for making wise ones because of their impact on us and on those we love. So as we sail through life, we choose our focus. We can either open our deck chair on the front of the ship to see where we're going, or we can place it on the back and see only where we've been.

Looking back can be positive in some cases. Cherished memories of family and friends bring joy. Recalling extraordinary individuals or inspirational stories brings strength and encouragement to persevere when the going gets tough. Remembering a hilarious incident adds sparkle to our perspective.

But when looking back on a negative past becomes our focus, we run into trouble. The Bible tells about a woman who did just that. And boy, oh boy, did she pay the price! Meet Mrs. Lot—the lady who cast an infamous backward glance. Hers is quite the story.

Mrs. Lot and her husband had settled in Sodom. One day God decided that He'd seen enough of Sodom's evil. He made plans to blow the city and its citizens into oblivion, but first, He sent two angels to rescue Mrs. Lot and her family. They literally seized their hands and rushed them to safety outside the city. "Run for your lives," they warned. "Do not stop anywhere in the valley. And *don't look back!* Escape to the mountains or you will die" (Genesis 19:16-17).

Mrs. Lot doesn't say much as the drama unfolds, but one sentence in the Bible speaks volumes: "Lot's wife looked back as she was following along behind him, and she became a pillar of salt" (verse 26).

The angels had commanded, "Run for your lives, do not stop, and DON'T LOOK BACK!" But Mrs. Lot failed to obey God's words. Perhaps she thought the orders didn't apply to her. Perhaps she thought she could sneak a peek without anyone noticing. Or maybe she couldn't bear the thought of leaving her past behind. We will never know what caused her to steal her backward glance that morning, but we *do* know what happened when she did, and it wasn't a pretty picture.

Liz Curtis Higgs, author of *Bad Girls of the Bible,* says that God took her by the hand many times in her young adult years and tried to lead her away from her destructive lifestyle. She says He urged her "not to look back but to press on to something better." How did she respond?

DEALING WITH UNFORGIVENESS

When someone offends us through word or deed, we often retaliate by harboring bitterness or nursing a grudge. However, saying goodbye to the ghosts in our past is impossible if we refuse to forgive.

Some women believe that forgiveness means excusing the offense. That's mistaken thinking. Forgiveness is neither condoning wrong behavior nor pretending that the offender did not hurt us.

Rather, forgiveness is actually acknowledging that a wrong was committed and that it caused pain (if it hadn't, there would be no need to forgive). It's a choice, an act of the will not to avenge evil with evil, but to obey God's command: "You must make allowance for each other's faults and forgive the person who offends you. Remember, the Lord forgave you, so you must forgive others" (Colossians 3:13).

Who benefits when we forgive our offenders? We do. The offender might never express remorse, but our forgiveness opens the door for our healing to begin.

I didn't believe him. I didn't trust him. I liked my pitiful party lifestyle and my apartment full of stuff—most of which has since been thrown out or sold at a yard sale for a quarter. What was I hanging on to? Why, at the last minute, so close to a clean, new life in Christ, did I turn back toward death again? And again? Stubborn pride. Foolish youth. Willful disobedience.[2]

I agree with Liz's list. And as I ponder it, I believe that at the root of these attitudes lies fear. God wants to take our hands and rescue us from the past with its regrets and bitterness and unforgiveness, but fear gets in the way.

We're not sure what new beginnings will look like. We don't know what change might cost us. Rather than slip our hand into His and face our fear, we insist on living life our way because it's what we know best. And—here's the big one—we don't understand His unfailing love for us.

Perhaps fear was the driving force behind Mrs. Lot's backward glance. After all, God's judgment on Sodom signaled the end to everything she held dear—her home, her friendships, her favorite day spa, her favorite coffee shop, yada yada. Familiarity provided so-called security, albeit deadly to her soul, and giving it up was frightening. Sue Augustine comments on this dynamic:

> Although we truly want to grow, develop, and move forward, most of us are not fond of endings because it normally means giving up old habits, past thinking patterns, former relationships, comfortable conditions, familiar attitudes, or established behaviors. However, endings are a part of life…We can respond with sadness, disappointment, bitterness, hostility, irritation, spite, or other feelings of ill will that can eventually bring on depression, anxiety, or despair. Or, we can refuse to hold tightly to our past, relinquishing all reactions that will harm us, rob us of joy, and put us into a state of distress.[3]

Mrs. Lot hung on tightly to her past, and doing so ended her life. Forever she'll be known as a human saltshaker. Hers is undeniably a unique claim to fame, but for all the wrong reasons. Unlike Mrs. Lot, the New Testament missionary Paul placed his deck chair on the front of the cruise ship. No one would have blamed him for clinging to his past. After all, he'd earned more credentials and diplomas than most of his peers would dare to wish for. His was an impressive résumé. But one glimpse of God's brilliance and power knocked him to his knees and put his life into proper perspective (Acts 9:3-6). Paul later said to the believers at Philippi, "I am focusing all my energies on this one thing: Forgetting the past and looking forward to what lies ahead, I strain to reach the end of the race and receive the prize for which God, through Christ Jesus, is calling us up to heaven" (Philippians 3:13-14).

Once Paul had experienced God's greatness and understood His call upon his life, nothing else mattered. He became a follower of Jesus Christ, dedicated to sharing the Good News with the world. Rather than looking back on the atrocities he'd committed while persecuting Christians, he received forgiveness and focused on pleasing the One who'd died to make forgiveness possible. Rather than relying on past accomplishments, he pressed forward to participate in God's purposes for his life from that point on.

If an acquaintance was asked to describe you or me, would she say we're most like Mrs. Lot, fearful of relinquishing the past, or Paul, focusing our energies on forgetting the past and looking forward to what lies ahead? I pray it's the latter. I hope you do too.

So, my dear reader, if you've already opened your deck chair at the front of the ship—bravo! If not, perhaps the time is now. I guarantee the view from the front is much nicer!

Ghost Busters

"Compulsively rehearsing the past is common to the human condition, especially if we feel we've failed in a significant way," says Myrna Hill, a licensed marriage and family therapist.[4]

When clients come to Myrna, she helps them see their issue in bite-sized bits so they can deal with each piece appropriately. The initial step to moving beyond one's past is to discuss what's happened and determine whether or not one is ready to deal with the subsequent pain of facing it.

For example, a woman who's had an affair must decide whether she's willing to encounter the pain that will come from confessing to her husband and facing the possible loss of her marriage. The mere thought of that scenario will almost certainly produce fear, but she will never experience freedom until she goes there. If she chooses to tolerate the ghost rather than face the pain of dealing with it honestly, she'll remain stuck—unable to find freedom from her past and unable to move forward into a future based in trust and truth.

Popular author Francine Rivers had an abortion when she was in college. Afraid of what others would think of her, she kept her secret for three decades. During that time, memories haunted her, and bad dreams stalked her sleep.

"For years I carried a heavy burden of guilt, fear, and shame," says Francine. "I lived with a horrible inner cancer. I didn't want to discuss or think about it. Healing came only after I acknowledged what I had done. I confessed it as sin committed against a holy God and received His forgiveness."

Confession marked the beginning of Francine's restoration. Her healing journey continued as she admitted her past to others, participated in postabortion classes, and allowed herself to grieve her lost child.

"My freedom came when I admitted, 'This is what I did. This is what it did to my life,'" says Francine. "Even though I'd placed my faith in Jesus Christ, years passed before I trusted Him with my private, excruciating pain. But God forgives. God restores. We must give Him our burden. When we grasp the depth of His love and mercy, we experience healing and restoration."[5]

After we confess the truth of what has happened, a second important element to finding freedom comes in defining the difference between guilt, shame, and shame's verbal sister, self-blame, and then dealing with each appropriately.

Guilt is good, says Myrna. It's God's way of telling us when we've done something wrong. If we're guilty for something we've done, we need to confess and repent—change direction, turn away from doing wrong, and turn back to God—and accept His forgiveness. "If we confess our sins to him, he is faithful and just to forgive us and to cleanse us from every wrong" (1 John 1:9).

Shame, on the other hand, is *not* good. It attacks our very essence, our sense of being. This is often instilled when we're children. If, as kids, we receive negative messages from a parent or caregiver, or if we lack a loving and accepting maternal presence, we will grow up questioning whether we're worthy of another's love and wondering whether we can trust other people. That lack of trust and feeling of unworthiness is later transferred to our relationship with God.

Repeating and internalizing the negative shame messages we receive from others results in self-blame. We feed ourselves untruths such as these:

Something is wrong with me.

Nobody really likes me—not even God.

I'll never get it right.

I'm not good enough.

This negative event is entirely my fault.

As long as we feed ourselves these negatives messages, we remain stuck. Moving forward involves acknowledging the vulnerable shamed places in our hearts, understanding their source, and admitting the subsequent pain we feel rather than denying or stuffing these emotions inside. Grieving this deep pain begins the process of healing.

It also requires learning to pour out our hearts to God and expecting Him to heal us. That too takes time—a somewhat foreign concept in our rush-rush world. Like Mary, we need to practice sitting in silence at Jesus' feet, resting in His love, and listening to His voice.

A third essential for freedom is the renewal of our minds. Shame and self-blame convince us that we're messed up and beyond hope of redemption. We can easily replay that message until it's embedded like concrete in our brains and we begin to behave in like manner.

God's Word, on the other hand, speaks the truth: Redemption is possible because the blood of Jesus cleanses us from *all* sin—the sins we've committed as well as those committed against us (1 John

---

HOW TO SLAY THE SHAME AND SELF-BLAME MONSTERS

1. Acknowledge to God that Christ has forgiven all your sins, even the ones that haunt you.

2. Recognize that your continuing feelings of shame and self-blame do not come from God.

3. If you are a concrete person, write down the self-blame messages you repeat to yourself and set the paper afire as an offering to God. If you are visual, imagine yourself lifting your burden of shame, setting it down in the arms of Jesus, and walking away. The idea is to establish a specific point at which you placed the shame and self-blame burden where it belongs—in the strong arms of the Savior.

4. When the feelings of shame return and the self-blame messages begin to replay, recall the fact of your forgiveness. *Father, I am forgiven and loved. Help me refuse shame and self-blame over an issue Christ has already dealt with.* Put your burden back in Jesus' arms.

5. Understand that knowing a truth doesn't make the feelings go away immediately. That takes practice, practice, practice. "The mature...by constant use have trained themselves to distinguish good from evil" (Hebrews 5:14 NIV).[6]

1:7). Scripture reassures us of God's unfailing love over and over and over again.

The story of the prodigal son is one illustration. The young man sowed his wild oats and then returned home after adding a ton of black smears to his personal record. But that didn't matter to his father. When Dad saw his son approach, he rose from his seat, *ran* to him, and embraced him.

That's the kind of God we have—one who loves us unconditionally. He doesn't love us as we should be; He loves us as we are. *He's* the one who invites us to come to Him and find rest for our souls. I wonder where you and I might be if God said, "I'm here for you, lady, but only after you get your act together." Thankfully that's not the case.

Finding freedom from the ghosts of our past is not an overnight trip. It's a time-consuming and often painful journey, but one that's worth the effort. In this context, the well-known phrase "no pain, no gain" is accurate indeed.

MaryAnne's Story

MaryAnne—"Mac"—grew up in a churchgoing family, the middle of five children. She was her dad's "baby doll," and she adored him in return. His sudden death when she was only 14 years old sent her into a personal tailspin.

Eighteen months later, Mac became pregnant. She married her baby's father and had a second child six years later. Unfortunately, Mac's husband was unfaithful, emotionally abusive, and addicted to alcohol and drugs. The couple separated after ten years. Tragically, he was murdered a short time later.

Mac remarried a year later and gave birth to a third child before her first wedding anniversary. That relationship mirrored the first and ended in divorce 13 years after the couple said "I do." This time Mac waited three years before marrying again. Thinking herself wiser, she married a man who called himself a Christian, but this marriage was more disappointing than the other two. After seven years of enduring her husband's angry outbursts and emotional abuse, she fled for safe shelter to a cottage overlooking the ocean.

As Mac gazed out the window toward the unending expanse of water, waves of shame and self-blame overwhelmed her: *I'm a failure...I'm a lousy wife...I'm a bad mother...Everything is my fault.* She'd always considered herself a steely survivor in the toughest of times, but now she broke. For the first time in two decades, she allowed herself to cry. The floodgates opened, and the tears flowed. And flowed. And flowed. And God began to heal Mac's life.

Face the past, He said. *Recognize what you've done and the need to change direction. I have a better way.* As the days passed in solitude, Mac found the courage to do as He said. She acknowledged the choices she'd made, the abuse, and the self-demeaning talk. And as she did, she began understanding the root cause behind her first pregnancy and subsequent unhealthy relationships: She feared being alone.

As a young girl, Mac had reveled in her dad's love and companionship. His death left her with a void that she tried to fill through the affections of other men. She jumped into marriage, albeit with abusive men, to squelch her fear of being alone.

"Weeping may go on all night, but joy comes with the morning," says Mac, referring to Psalm 30:5. "That verse describes what happened. Facing my past with all its abuse and brokenness caused immense grief. At times I could barely breathe, but God brought me through and turned my sorrow into joy."

Actually, God did even more than that! He taught her that having a personal relationship with Jesus Christ was more important than simply having a church background and an academic understanding about Him. She discovered the joy of speaking with Him as she would to a friend and of sensing His presence with her every moment of the day.

Imagine Mac's surprise when, four years later, God planted her in the most notorious section of the inner city and, as He did with Jana Lapel, turned her into a strong and graceful oak for His glory.

In 2004, when a bad winter storm whipped through the area, she asked the pastor of a local church to open the facility to provide shelter for the homeless. He handed her the keys and said, "You're responsible for my building while you're here."

That experience birthed Nightshift Ministry. Mac gave up her career in sales and marketing and began living off her personal savings to work with the homeless, with girls on the street and folks addicted to heroin, crack, and crystal meth. Within two years, more than 200 people from 30 churches volunteered to help cook and serve 150 to 200 meals per night for the homeless.

Mac's enthusiasm is contagious as she credits God for saving her from total despair and the fear of being alone. She's no longer haunted by her past. She's joy-filled, confident, and completely fulfilled in her relationship with Jesus Christ.

"Isaiah 61:1 describes my life," says Mac. "The Spirit of the Sovereign LORD is upon me, because the LORD has appointed me to bring good news to the poor. He has sent me to comfort the brokenhearted and to announce that captives will be released and prisoners will be freed."[7]

Mac is free, and now she plays a role in helping others discover freedom too. What an amazing testimony to God's desire and ability to give us victory over our past!

Focus on the Future

As I mentioned earlier, every person on the face of the earth has a past—even the 12 disciples of Christ who walked with Him on earth 2000 years ago. Consider Matthew, the tax collector. He undoubtedly fixed and fudged numbers to stash a few extra coins in his pockets. What about Simon the Zealot? Apparently he hung out with a political group with a reputation for violence.

Yes, Christ chose an interesting bunch of characters to play on His team. None had received the Citizen of the Year award. None had won elections or been recognized as celebrities. They were just ordinary guys with a few splotches in their past. But that didn't bother Jesus.

Scripture bears no mention of Jesus publicly referring to His team's past failures as they worked, prayed, ate, and slept together. That just wasn't His style. He was more interested in focusing on what they could become. Gordon MacDonald points this out:

> Jesus took that first group and turned them into kingdom champions. No one was beyond redemption, beyond the possibility of life change… While His disciples tended to be glued to the past and the present, Jesus focused on the future. He saw every incident, conversation, and learning experience in light of future maturity.[8]

By the Holy Spirit's power, the disciples were transformed into dynamic miracle workers willing to be martyred for Christ's sake, men whose passion and perseverance laid the foundation for Christianity around the world today.

That thought should bring huge consolation to us! However scarred or marred our past is, we don't have to stay there. God has better things in store. " 'For I know the plans I have for you,' says the Lord. 'They are plans for good and not for disaster, to give you a future and a hope' " (Jeremiah 29:11). Yes, our past experiences shape and influence who we are, but they don't have to control who we become.

Donna's Story

Abuse of every sort turned Donna into a woman who felt ugly and unlovable. Afraid of rejection if others knew her past, she avoided conversations and eye contact. She struggled with depression and suicidal thoughts. She hid behind the security of her home, her husband, and the busyness of work and church ministry.

While Donna remained glued to her past, God focused on her future. Time and time again, He spoke to her through His Word.

Donna responded by typing out the verses and posting them above her desk where she could see them often.

One day she mustered the courage to ask, *God, do You love me?* The reply came: *I have loved you with an everlasting love.*

Curious, Donna studied her concordance to see if God had ever spoken those words. Sure enough, she found Jeremiah 31:3-4. "Long ago the LORD said to Israel: 'I have loved you, my people, with an everlasting love. With unfailing love I have drawn you to myself. I will rebuild you, my virgin Israel. You will again be happy and dance merrily with tambourines.'" Donna claimed those verses as God's promise. She chose to believe that He would indeed rebuild her life. And He kept His promise.

The journey took time. Donna immersed herself in God's Word, sought professional counseling, and used antidepressants for several months. The combination worked. Donna no longer hides behind busyness to avoid people. Now she's attending a university to earn her masters degree in counseling![9]

We tend to dwell on the past; God wants us to move forward. He wants to lift us from the quicksand of our mistakes and put our feet on solid ground so we can dance unhindered.

> I waited patiently for the LORD to help me,
>   and he turned to me and heard my cry.
> He lifted me out of the pit of despair,
>   out of the mud and the mire.
> He set my feet on solid ground
>   and steadied me as I walked along.
> He has given me a new song to sing,
>   a hymn of praise to our God.
> Many will see what he has done and be astounded.
>   They will put their trust in the LORD (Psalm 40:1-4).

Warning: Change Coming

Scripture tells the story of a man whose body was paralyzed for

38 years. When Jesus saw him, He asked a strange question: "Do you want to be healed?" The answer would seem obvious, wouldn't it? Maybe. Then again, maybe not.

Being healed from paralysis would mean a lifestyle shift for this man. He might be expected to get a job. He'd have to assume responsibility for his own well-being rather than relying on others to care for him. He didn't know how family and friends would respond to him if he suddenly became well.

Jesus' words first challenged him to consider the cost of achieving physical wholeness. And then Jesus told the man to do the impossible: "Stand up, pick up your sleeping mat, and walk!" (John 5:8). The paralyzed man made his choice—he believed and obeyed. New life poured into his limbs, and he began to walk.

Sometimes our past failures paralyze us emotionally and spiritually. Breaking free means change, and change isn't always comfortable, especially when it means revisiting pain. But healing is available through Jesus Christ. He can do the impossible, and He wants to. He is ready to exchange our paralysis with new life. The choice is ours.

Stand up and walk!

✦ POINTS FOR PROGRESS ✦

Have mercy on me, O God,
  because of your unfailing love.
Because of your great compassion,
  blot out the stain of my sins.
Wash me clean from my guilt.
  Purify me from my sin.
For I recognize my shameful deeds—
  they haunt me day and night (Psalm 51:1-3).

1. King David wrote these words. To what sin was he referring? (See 2 Samuel 11.) What words indicate his

personal struggle with the ghost of his past? How can you relate?

2. To what aspect of God's character was David appealing when he prayed this prayer?

3. Sometimes we feel as though we must do penance for our sins. How do these verses refute that thinking? What washes us clean from our sin?

4. Philippians 4:8 says, "Fix your thoughts on what is true and honorable and right. Think about things that are pure and lovely and admirable. Think about things that are excellent and worthy of praise." How does this verse compare to the thoughts that prevail when the ghost of our past is haunting us?

5. If you struggle with self-blame, negative memories, or unforgiveness, write the issue on a piece of paper and then burn or shred it. Confess your inability to move beyond the past. Thank the Lord that, through His forgiveness and by His strength, the ghosts of your past have no power over your future.

✦ PROMISES TO PONDER ✦

So now there is no condemnation for those who belong to Christ Jesus. For the power of the life-giving Spirit has freed you through Christ Jesus from the power of sin that leads to death...God destroyed sin's control over us by giving his Son as a sacrifice for our sins...Those who are dominated by the sinful nature think about sinful things, but those who are controlled by the Holy Spirit think about things that please the Spirit. If your sinful nature controls your mind, there is death. But if the Holy Spirit controls your mind, there is life and peace (Romans 8:1-3,5-6).

I am about to do a brand-new thing. See, I have already begun! Do you not see it? I will make a pathway through the wilderness for my people to come home. I will create rivers for them in the desert...Yes, I will make springs in the desert, so that my chosen people can be refreshed. I have made Israel for myself, and they will someday honor me before the whole world (Isaiah 43:19-21).

Surely the Lord has done great things! Don't be afraid, my people! Be glad now and rejoice because the Lord has done great things. Don't be afraid, you animals of the field! The pastures will soon be green. The trees will again be filled with luscious fruit; fig trees and grape-vines will flourish once more. Rejoice, you people of Jerusalem! Rejoice in the Lord your God! For the rains he sends are an expression of his grace. Once more the autumn rains will come, as well as the rains of spring. The threshing floors will again be piled high with grain, and the presses will overflow with wine and olive oil. The Lord says, "I will give you back what you lost to the stripping locusts, the cutting locusts, the swarming locusts, and the hopping locusts" (Joel 2:20-25).

✦ PRAYING THE PROMISES ✦

Father, thank You for giving me freedom from condemnation! Thank You for giving me freedom from the power of sin through the work of Jesus Christ. I pray that Your Holy Spirit will fully control me and that, as a result, my thoughts would not ponder the sinful things of my past but focus only on those things that please You. Death has no part in my life. I commit my mind to the Holy Spirit and embrace life and peace. In Jesus' name. Amen.

Dear God, thank You for promising to do a brand-new thing in my life. Remove every trace of past failures and fill my life with a renewed sense of Your presence and goodness. Open my eyes to recognize Your hand at work in me and on my behalf. Create rivers of living water where dust and dry bones once were. Make springs in the desert. Refresh my spirit, Lord. I'm Your daughter—use my life to bring honor to Your glorious name. Amen.

Dear Father, thank You for doing new and great things in my life. Because of Your great love for me, I will not be afraid of voices from my past. I will not dwell on the wasted years or the damage the locusts have done. Rather, I will rejoice in who You are and in Your promises to restore me. Pour the autumn and spring rains over me, Lord. Be pleased to bear much fruit in and through my life. Amen.

9

It's Not About Gray Hair and Wrinkles

*To fear is one thing. To let fear grab you by the
tail and swing you around is another.*

KATHERINE PATERSON

My calendar shows four health-related appointments this month. The first was a regular dental checkup. "The next time you come, I'll crown one back molar and start replacing your old fillings," said the dentist. "Eventually you'll need your six upper crowns replaced, and after that we'll crown the lower front six teeth."

I winced inwardly at the thought of whirring drills. But that concern dissipated minutes later as I entered the hospital for my next appointment—my annual mammogram.

The attendant reminded me of a guard from a WWII concentration camp. "Strip to the waist," she commanded as she typed my name into her computer.

I followed her orders.

"Now step over here and place your breast on this panel," she barked.

I obeyed again. And as I did, a recent e-mail popped into my mind. I couldn't resist the temptation to tell the sergeant about it.

"Hey—did you hear about the woman who wanted to prepare herself for her first mammogram?" I asked.

No response. I barreled ahead anyway.

"She stepped into her garage at three a.m., when the temperature of the cement floor was perfect. Then she took off her pajama top and positioned herself on the ground with one breast under the rear tire of her car. A friend slowly backed up the car until her breast was flattened and chilled. Then she rolled over and went through the same thing with her other breast. When she was finished, she said, 'That was fun! Let's do it again next year at this time!'"

"We're done. Get dressed," she ordered.

A week later I visited my eye doctor. The good news: no glaucoma. The bad news: It's time for bifocals. For the past year, I've felt like a mad scientist or an antique something-or-other, peering over my cheap reading glasses at my kids, my husband, and my audiences. It's time to do something more convenient. And so, having been born in 1958, necessity overrules vanity. My arm is too short and my vision too blurred for me to care about whether or not I look good in glasses.

My fourth appointment is yet to come. My family doctor plans to remove a suspicious-looking mole from my leg and send it for a biopsy. "I'll eat my hat if it's melanoma," she said when she examined it several days ago. "But there's a good possibility it's basal cell carcinoma."

The mere mention of the word *melanoma* made my heart skip a beat. Our camp director—a healthy 62-year-old man—was diagnosed with melanoma last year. He lived only ten months despite undergoing surgery and chemotherapy.

I left the doctor's office and climbed into my car for the ride home. As I drove, I thought about my aging body. Cellulite and blue veins decorate my legs. Gray streaks highlight my hair. Love handles hold up my pants. And arthritis slows my joints.

There's no denying it. I'm getting older. I must be—I can actually appreciate the humor in jokes about aging. Take this poem that appeared in my e-mail, for instance:

SENIOR CITIZENS ARE VALUABLE

We are more valuable
than any of the younger generations:
We have silver in our hair.
We have gold in our teeth.
We have stones in our kidneys.
We have lead in our feet.
And we are loaded with natural gas!

Silver—check. Gold—check. Stones—check. Lead? Gas? Check, check. My mind insists I'm still 23, but reality says otherwise. I'm older now than my mother was when I considered her ancient. Among the college-age counselors who work at our camp, I'm viewed as an "older woman." When I enter a room that's filled to capacity, young people stand up and offer me their chairs. Where has my youth gone? And what does the future hold as time transports me toward my senior years?

I watch my parents and in-laws struggle with aging and its related issues—nursing homes, cancer treatments, Parkinson's disease, mental confusion, loss of appetite, sleeplessness, and total dependence on caregivers. I admire their courage as they travel a difficult and trying road, but I must admit that I hope my destiny takes a different direction. But that's not really my choice, is it? The aging process is a fact of life, and only God knows the specifics that lie ahead.

Yet, as I travel the journey, I *do* have a choice regarding my perspective. I can either let fear grip me and fight the inevitable, or I can accept aging with an attitude that says, *Bring it on! The best is yet to come!*

Attitude Check

Is it any wonder that the subject of aging often brings groans and moans? After all, it's associated with life-altering health problems such as strokes and heart attacks. It occasionally includes painful transitions such as moving from the family home into an extended-care facility, living apart from one's spouse, or attending the funerals of peers who pass away first. It carries the fear of losing one's independence—a driver's license, perhaps—or being considered incompetent by others. And it also brings the fear of losing one's mental capacity.

Several years ago, we listened to a couple tell about caring for the man's mother, who had developed Alzheimer's. They'd brought her into their home and tried to make her as comfortable as possible in her new surroundings. One afternoon, she snuck out of the house. The daughter-in-law grew frantic when she realized the older woman had disappeared, and she ran outside to search the woods behind the home. There she found her mother-in-law banging her head on a tree and crying in despair. Her words indicated that she was aware her mind was no longer working properly. What a heartache!

There's no doubt about it. Aging brings challenges, and their impact on us is often determined by our attitude toward them. According to the *Journal of Personality and Social Psychology,* Yale researcher Becca R. Levy and her colleagues found that adults who maintained positive attitudes toward aging lived more than seven years longer than their peers with negative outlooks. The study investigated 660 adults between ages 50 and 94 in Ohio and tracked them for 22 years. The participants' attitudes about aging were gauged according to statements such as, "Everything gets worse as I get older" and "I have as much pep as last year."[1]

Denying the fact that we're growing older only hurts us. It robs us, and others, of the potential placed within us by a God who has designed us for a purpose and rules sovereignly over our lives from beginning to end.

Have you ever seen a 60-something woman dress in clothing designed for the younger set, dye her hair, and try to camouflage her wrinkles with way too much makeup? One woman might do this as an expression of her flamboyant personality, but another might be afraid of aging and trying to stall the process by pretending to be someone she's not. By succumbing to that fear, she denies herself the joy of living in the present moment, and she denies others the beauty of her true self.

We're all growing older. It's inevitable. If we're not, we have only one option, right? And so, as the candles on our birthday cake increase year by year, we're faced with a choice: to be fearful and fight the aging process, or to face our fears by accepting and even embracing it.

Accepting the fact that we're growing older means we feel comfortable with the gray hairs. We can laugh when the fairy tale saying "not by the hair of my chinny-chin-chin" assumes a whole new meaning. We can thank God for daily strength and enjoy whatever we're able to do physically despite the inevitable leaks and creaks.

Embracing aging is a level beyond mere acceptance. Cecil Murphey says that it means to recognize and delight in the advantages of growing older. He evaluated the aging process in his own life and then shared these insights:

> I focused on aging as a positive factor in my life. If God planned for us to get older, why should I argue and call this phase of life negative? Is it possible, I asked myself, that God intended the last years to be the best? Instead of slinking into oblivion, could the divine plan encourage us to sing the hymns of triumph all the way to the grave? Can it be that God wants us to enjoy our final part of the journey as much as we did the first two parts? Perhaps enjoy it even more?
>
> I decided the answer was a resounding yes. My task was to learn to live by embracing this final, triumphant phase of my life.[2]

Cecil's attitude is one we should all strive to adopt. But how can we develop and maintain it? By understanding that the presence of the eternal God goes with us, and He holds our days in His hands.

That truth, when we internalize it, brings courage to face physical and emotional pain, strength to face seemingly impossible tasks, and stability in life's changing seasons.

God Himself gives us a promise worth memorizing and recalling each time the fear of growing old creeps in: "I created you and have cared for you since before you were born. I will be your God throughout your lifetime—until your hair is white with age. I made you, and I will care for you. I will carry you along and save you" (Isaiah 46:3-4). What a beautiful reminder—we're held in the hand of a God who created us and cares for us throughout our entire lives. Even when we're too old to care for ourselves, He assumes responsibility for us. That doesn't mean we'll never encounter trials that go hand in hand with old age, but it does mean we can rest in His presence and love as He leads us through every season, all the way to the grand finale.

And speaking of a grand finale, picture this: Canada celebrates its birthday on July 1. Each year when that day draws to a close, our community gathers at a beach to watch fireworks. With every boom and bang, vibrant colors explode and splash across the sky. They spiral and sparkle and spin before disappearing into the sea. It's an amazing 15-minute display. But the best part—the finale—comes last. The fireworks explode in rapid succession and paint the sky with a mosaic that leaves onlookers oohing and aahing in amazement.

Old age is often considered to be the season in which we lose the fizzle of our lives, but that need not be so. When we walk with God, holding fast to His promised love and presence, it can be the grand finale, impacting those around us for good.

The journey itself may not guarantee a heap of laughter and good times, but we can soften it with an upbeat perspective. Here are several positive opportunities that accompany the natural aging process.

Make Peace with Our Bodies

Without a doubt, time and age change most bodies. My wedding gown hangs in our storage room. Modeling it would be fun, but unfortunately, a few things—my arms, hips, and waistline—have changed in the 25 years since I wore it last. It would take a magical shrinking act to squish me into it today.

And then there's the three-B issue: bathing suits, bras, and blue jeans. I actually enjoyed shopping for them once upon a time, but now they're at the bottom of my "fun things to buy" list. I'm convinced that today's clothing designers have a conspiracy against women over 29. They're probably in cahoots with the folks who manufacture mirrors for department-store dressing rooms. For some reason, I have difficulty looking in the mirror and recognizing myself as the woman who's looking back.

I feel like a gal who went for her yearly physical. The nurse asked her how much she weighed. She answered, "One hundred and fifteen pounds." When she stepped onto the scale, however, it registered 150.

"What's your height?" asked the nurse.

"I'm five-eight," answered the woman.

The nurse measured her. "Actually, you're five-five," she said. Then she took the woman's blood pressure. She gave a whistle and exclaimed, "It's very high!"

"Of course it's high!" the woman shouted. "When I came in here, I was tall and slender! Now I'm short and fat!"

I laugh, but I can understand where the poor woman's coming from. Once smooth and toned, my body has assumed an appearance all its own. Maybe you can relate. The natural inclination is to balk at its betrayal. But unless that appearance is a direct result of improper nutrition and lack of exercise, it doesn't have to be a negative.

One writer in her fifties shared her insights:

> The older body is not beautiful in the irrefutable way of the young, but it is beautifully particular. With each year, the female body cultivates its own dialect, distinct from the signals broadcast by the young and flawless body. I

rather like to see the bodies of my female friends age, because the changes become less a departure from the ideal than an expression of their own peculiar selves.[3]

Embracing the aging process and accepting our changing body grants us the ability to feel comfortable in our skin. It frees us from the pressure of comparing ourselves to youth's unrealistic physical ideals. Rather than trying to measure up to an unattainable standard, we can relax and accept our body as an old friend who has carried us through life's ups and downs. For example, for several years following the cesarean delivery of my second child, I bemoaned my abdominal scar and loss of muscle tone. Today I don't mind that my abdomen doesn't lie flat—I consider its scar and shape as trophies of motherhood and marks of God's faithfulness through a difficult time. It's all in one's perspective.

Aging and its related challenges also give us opportunities to appreciate our bodies for what they do rather than for what they look like. Youth cares more about appearance, but maturity recognizes the intricacies of design and how God has fearfully and wonderfully shaped our cells, skin, and organs to function. Imagine the brains and creativity it took to put us together! What an amazing God we serve!

Several of my friends have battled breast cancer. Some grieved the loss of a breast and the impact of a mastectomy on their feelings of femininity, but they grew in their appreciation of the way God designed bodies to attack enemy cells, heal after major surgery, and grow new hair, albeit black and curly!

Aging bodies are positive factors in our lives in another way too. In a society that puts undue emphasis on physical beauty and strength, gray hair and wrinkles remind us that life is more than good looks and great shape. The marks of maturity cause us to reevaluate our priorities, and they remind us that God sees the heart. He values character above physical attractiveness, and so should we.

Offer Encouragement to Other Women

Older women might have a hard time winning a beauty pageant, but when it comes to life experience, there's no contest. They've lived long enough to feel both hope and disappointment many times. They've suffered failure and attained success. They've figured out what works, what doesn't, and why. If they've maintained a teachable spirit and allowed God to shape their character, they have much to offer other women.

Lynn's life reflects this truth. She was born in 1946. She lost her mother at age 22, one year prior to her wedding. Her mom's death left a void, but several mature Christian women came alongside to encourage her in her new role as a wife and homemaker. They coached her in practical skills such as cooking and crocheting and gave tips for developing consistent and meaningful devotions. Their influence planted the seed that blossomed into her lifelong passion for mentoring other women.

Through the years, Lynn has quietly taken younger women under her wing, meeting one-on-one with those wanting to learn to cook, study the Bible, or memorize Scripture. She has also launched church programs that bring women of all ages together for fellowship and encouragement. She teaches a Sunday school class that spans three generations. As someone who has stayed happily married for nearly 40 years, raised three children, survived cancer, and experienced a treasure chest of ups and downs, she possesses a wealth of wisdom and knowledge for the younger generation. Women are drawn to her because they sense her genuine concern for their well-being.

To Lynn's delight, the Lord has given her opportunity to influence another cross-section of women—immigrants and refugees. She recently completed a course that qualifies her to teach English as a second language. Combining that with her gift of hospitality, she opens her home to women of other nationalities. She gives language lessons, teaches cooking classes, and even hosts birthday parties. Doing so builds relationships and gives opportunities to share Christ's love in practical ways. She recently taught a Burmese woman how to make blackberry jam. In response, the woman said, "Thank you for letting me into your kitchen. Not everyone wants to share their kitchen with me."

Lynn says every stage of her life has been exciting, but this is the most exciting yet. She believes she's doing what God has created her to do, and she says she's totally fulfilled. Obviously those receiving her encouragement agree—her home hums with happy activity as women come and go.[4]

Some folks feel that age widens the generation gap, but that needn't be true. Using wisdom gleaned through the aging process, we can build bridges and encourage those who have yet to travel as many miles as we have. Besides, according to God's Word, this is our responsibility: "These older women must train the younger women to love their husbands and their children, to live wisely and be pure, to take care of their homes, to do good, and to be submissive to their husbands. Then they will not bring shame on the word of God" (Titus 2:4-5).

If you're feeling old and washed-up, think again. Ask the Lord to help you recognize the treasures you have to share. Ask Him for opportunities to invest those jewels in a younger woman's life. If your heart is open to doing whatever He asks, you'll be amazed at the answer!

Leave a Legacy for Coming Generations

At 60 years of age, Lynn has experienced God's faithfulness in numerous ways. For instance, her husband's career changes have meant several moves to new locations. In each case, God has provided the housing, friends, and church families they needed.

When one of her sons sensed God's leading to overseas missionary service in a country closed to the Gospel, she experienced God's peace as she said goodbye and released him into His care.

When she was diagnosed with breast cancer, the Lord reassured her of His presence in an amazing way. At her first visit to the chemotherapy clinic, Lynn was treated by a Christian nurse who spoke about her favorite author whose work had been especially meaningful to her. She asked Lynn if she was familiar with his writings. Lynn laughed with delight—the author was her father! The connection formed an immediate bond and fused a lasting friendship between the two women.

Life experiences gained through time and the aging process have given Lynn the opportunity to experience God and prove His faithfulness over and over again. When she recalls these stories and others to her kids and grandkids, she's passing on a legacy of faith that will encourage them to trust the Lord when they encounter the tough stuff.

Someday our physical lives on earth will end. All our busyness will cease. All our stuff will be divided up, given away, sold, or tossed. When we're gone, what will we leave behind that really matters? And how will our family and friends remember us?

One woman's tombstone says, "No runs, no hits, just errors." Another says, "On the whole, I'd rather be antiquing." What will yours and mine say?

On my living room wall hangs a candid photo of my grandmother, taken about two years before she died at age 95. That picture speaks volumes to me. It shows my white-haired grandma reading her Bible—a discipline she practiced every morning until age and illness forced her to stop. I remember conversations in which she reassured me of her prayers for our family. As long as she was able, she spent huge portions of her day praying for each of her 33 grandchildren and 48 great-grandchildren by name. What a godly legacy she left for her descendants!

I referred to Caleb in a previous chapter. His legacy is a model worth noting. He was 45 years old when he spied out the promised land. He later recalled the event and said, "I returned and gave from my heart a good report, but my brothers who went with me frightened the people and discouraged them from entering the Promised Land. For my part, I followed the LORD my God completely" (Joshua 14:7-8).

This verse lends a great analogy to the theme of aging. Let's imagine ourselves at 45, looking down the road into the second half of our lives. Knowing God has promised to go with us and give us victory over every enemy in the territory, will we respond as the majority did, focusing on circumstances and cowering in fear, causing those who follow to fear as well? Or will we respond as Caleb did and wholly follow the Lord, giving a good report to those who come behind?

I pray that we'll follow Caleb's example. If ever there was a super senior, he was it. Here's what he said at 85:

> I am as strong now as I was when Moses sent me on that journey, and I can still travel and fight as well as I could then. So I'm asking you to give me the hill country that the LORD promised me. You will remember that as scouts we found the Anakites living there in great, walled cities. But if the LORD is with me, I will drive them out of the land, just as the LORD said (verses 11-12).

Caleb's legacy challenges me to look forward to the land that lies before me. I hope it does the same for you. We can navigate the aging process fully aware of its challenges but knowing that because the Lord is with us, we need not be afraid. That confidence enables us to give a good report from our hearts. And that good report will encourage those who follow us.

Caution: Bumps Ahead

Even though we want to focus on the positives of the aging process, we must admit that growing old presents challenges. Pain experts estimate that 40 percent of the U.S. population suffers some form of lingering pain severe enough to interfere with the quality of life. The causes range from cancer treatments to accident-related injuries, from arthritis to migraine headaches, but the leading culprit is age.

"People are getting older," says Dr. Allan Basbaum, a neuroscientist at the University of California. "And the older you get, the more likely it is that everything's going to go wrong."[5]

If we want to leave a good legacy, we need to respond to these challenges in an appropriate way. That doesn't mean we have to mask our struggles with a fake smile even when we're having a "terrible, horrible, no good, very bad day." Neither does it mean we should act like Ms. Tough Stuff when we're feeling as if we're dying on both the outside and the inside.

But it *does* mean being honest with those who care about our well-being without complaining about our circumstances or criticizing their efforts to help. And it *does* mean admitting our fears. It's okay to say, "The thought of undergoing a knee replacement terrifies me. Would you pray with me?"

If we consistently complain or cower in fear about what lies ahead, we not only taint the perspective of those who follow us but also sink ourselves deeper into the mire of despondency. If we focus on the Lord's presence in our lives, however, we find ourselves able to face each new day with renewed hope and inner strength.

Marjorie has found this to be true. At age 52, she has suffered chronic pain for 27 years. It began when a back injury at age 25 forced her to give up physical work and athletic activity. The pain intensified, and in 1994 a doctor diagnosed her with fibromyalgia.

Marjorie says that her life as a young woman had resembled a big smorgasbord, like a table spread with a feast of opportunities. Chronic pain snatched away the plates one by one. The challenge forced her to adapt.

Raised in a religious home environment, Marjorie had always

YOU KNOW YOU'RE GETTING OLDER WHEN...

Everything hurts, and what doesn't hurt doesn't work.

The gleam in your eye is from the sun hitting your bifocals.

Your back goes out more often than you do.

Dialing long distance wears you out.

You sink your teeth into a steak and they stay there.

considered prayer and church attendance as important elements of her life. But as her pain increased and lingered, prayer turned from rote recitation to a lifeline from which she drew supernatural strength. Church attendance, a discipline she'd practiced to please her parents and God, became a necessity that nourished her soul. Her thirst to know God increased. She began attending Bible studies, retreats, and workshops, and she started building relationships with other Christian women. Through it all, she began to understand God as a loving Father, not merely a God who was to be feared in a negative sense.

I met Marjorie several years ago. I believe she's always honest with me when I ask her how she's doing, but I've never heard her complain. Perhaps that's because her understanding of God's character has enabled her to rest in His care. As a result, she's learned to accept those things she cannot change and to trust His grace to see her through the dark days. She also credits her attitude to several other habits she has developed:

She reviews Scripture. She finds hope in the Beatitudes (Matthew 5:3-10) because they recall God's promises to His children. For instance, He says He will comfort those who mourn and reveal Himself to those who are pure in heart.

She chooses to think about others' needs. Rather than fixate on her own situation, she remembers those whose circumstances are more difficult than hers, including disabled seniors and children battling cancer.

She puts her mind in a different place. When pain threatens to overwhelm her, she pulls out her watercolor paints and an easel. She has to exercise caution, though, because overextending herself can increase discomfort.

She smiles at people. It sounds simple, and it is. If she sees someone who looks unhappy, she smiles, and if the moment seems right, she asks about her day. "Sometimes folks open up like a flower," says Marjorie. "They feel as though they've been acknowledged, and that changes their perspective. It doesn't always work, but why not try? Putting a smile on one person's face can cause a ripple effect, and I can do that even when I'm in pain. I may not be able to do some things, but there are a lot of things I *can* do."[6]

I'm grateful for women like Marjorie. Her journey has taken her down a bumpy road, and pain is her constant companion, but she reflects peace. She could have become embittered toward God, angry at her limitations, and jealous of women who are able to do more, but she has chosen a better way. Her attitude honors the Lord and blesses those who know her.

Another woman for whom I'm grateful is Judy. She knows what it means to face another bump in the journey—the loss of one's independence. And she's amazingly honest about the difficulty of accepting help from others graciously.

Judy was born with severely underdeveloped legs. She underwent corrective surgery at age ten, trading her "deformed footies for stumps" and metal stilts for artificial legs. Now in her sixties, my friend gets around by means of prosthetics or a wheelchair.

I asked Judy if she could share some insights about dealing with the loss of independence. "In all honesty, it's like being trapped or caged," she said. "We want to be can-do people. As soon as we can't do something, our self-worth is threatened, and our peace of mind disappears. I've been dealing with this for more than 60 years, and I'm still struggling."

On a recent plane trip to San Jose, Judy was asked to wait in her seat until the necessary equipment arrived to lower her and three other passengers from the aircraft to the tarmac. But in Judy's opinion, waiting for help seemed like an unnecessary evil. She strapped her purse around her neck, dropped to the floor, crawled down the aisle, and descended 20 steps to the tarmac, ignoring the flight attendants' pleas for her to get back in her seat.

"I don't have the patience to be disabled," said Judy as she ended her tale. "People might look at me and think I have a strong will, but actually, it's probably more of a struggle with the universal problem of pride. Admitting my need for help forces me to embrace my brokenness, and who wants to do that?"

SERENITY PRAYER
REINHOLD NIEBHUR

God, grant me the serenity
to accept the things I cannot change,
Courage to change the things I can,
And wisdom to know the difference.

Living one day at a time,
Enjoying one moment at a time,
Accepting hardships as a pathway
to peace,
Taking, as Jesus did, this sinful
world as it is,
Not as I would have it,
Trusting that You will make all
things right
If I surrender to Your will,
That I may be reasonably happy in
this life
And supremely happy with You
forever in the next.

Amen.

Thanks to a Christian counselor's advice, Judy is learning to do just that—embrace her brokenness. She's learning to remove her "strong victor" mask and be honest with family and friends about the frustrations she faces on a daily basis. She's also learning to admit her fears. As a result, she's experiencing newfound intimacy in relationships with those she loves.[7]

Judy's been discovering yet another truth amid the bumps in her journey: God tucks His glory in the least expected places, including the aging process. It's true—losing one's independence can bring embarrassment, feelings of isolation, fear of being mistreated, and fear of an unknown future. We can grow frustrated and angry at our inability to meet our own self-imposed high standards. We can become our own worst enemies by being intolerant of our decline. But into the darkness shines the light of God's glory as He cares for us through the hands of those willing and able to help, if we'll let them.

When the Doctor Makes a Mistake

Two women were discussing their recent surgeries. "I had an appendectomy last month," said one. "The doctor left a sponge in me by mistake."

"A sponge?" exclaimed the other. "Do you feel pain?"

"None," said the first woman. "But I'm always thirsty!"

This imaginary conversation brings a chuckle, but doctors' mistakes in real life are no laughing matter. We place our trust in the expertise of medical professionals, but unfortunately, they're only human. They work long, stress-filled hours. They get tired. Sometimes they make a wrong diagnosis or operate on the wrong limb. As we navigate the aging process, we find ourselves increasingly reliant upon doctors. But knowing that they can make mistakes, trusting them with our physical well-being can be a scary thing. How can we protect ourselves from medical errors, and how are we to respond if we experience them?

Janet Lynn Mitchell learned the hard way. She was a teenager when her surgeon cut one of her leg bones incorrectly. Then he tried to cover up his mistake with subsequent surgeries. Janet trusted him—until another doctor blew the whistle and told her the truth. Rage filled Janet's heart and mind when she realized that her pain and physical limitations were the direct result of fraud, not the congenital complication he'd fabricated.

Anger and unforgiveness threatened to overwhelm Janet for several years, but thankfully, God healed her perspective. He showed her that forgiveness was not optional, and that although choosing to forgive the doctor would not change her past, it would free her future. He also encouraged her to believe that He could bring good from evil.

Janet began wondering how she could prevent other patients from experiencing similar tragedy. When she discovered that medical malpractice is the eighth-leading cause of death in America, she knew she had to act.[8] She learned as much as possible about the medical profession and laws relating to it, and then she hired a lawyer to present her case in court. A decade-long battle ensued, and Janet won.[9]

In fact, the state of California signed Assembly Bill 2571 into law as a result of Janet's perseverance. This law says that California medical professionals can no longer alter medical records or withhold medical information, nor can they rely on the statute of limitations to protect them from investigation by the California Medical Board.

Was God able to bring good from evil? Absolutely. His promise to do so acts like a safety net for His children. Even when the doctor makes a mistake, we can rest assured that God is able to use it for our good and His glory: "And we know that God causes everything to work together for the good of those who love God and are called according to his purpose for them" (Romans 8:28). Part of that purpose is to become like Jesus. And that means exercising forgiveness toward those who hurt us, accidentally or otherwise.

But what about the nitty-gritty, hands-on aspects of protecting ourselves? Drawing from her personal experience, Janet insists that we know what our medical records say. In her case, people had deleted or altered vital information. She suggests that we research our doctor's professional history with the Medical Board. How long has he been practicing? What's his area of specialty? Has he ever been sued? If so, why? She also encourages patients to take an advocate to appointments and to ask questions if they're uncertain about something the doctors says. If you're struggling with fear related to your medical care, check out Janet's website www.janetlynnmitchell. com for more helpful tips, or read her book *Taking a Stand* (Green Key Books, 2006).

A Closing Thought

As I wrote this chapter, Gene and I spent three days visiting his mom in a nursing home. While there, I observed various seniors. Some were sweet and cooperative; others complained or shouted inappropriate comments. One threw wadded paper napkins at her peers sitting at her breakfast table.

The scenario challenged me to consider my attitude as I grow older and face changes over which I won't always have control. I believe one of the keys to maintaining a sweet spirit through the aging process is to cultivate a thankful heart today.

We can easily grumble when our bodies ache and creak. We can become discouraged when our health fails and we lose our independence. Having a thankful heart when circumstances are less than ideal is more difficult, but that's what God commands. And because of who He is, we have ample reason for doing so: "Be strong and courageous! Do not be afraid of them! *[including the challenges of old age]*. The LORD your God will go ahead of you. He will neither fail you nor forsake you" (Deuteronomy 31:6).

✦ POINTS FOR PROGRESS ✦

1. Eleanor Roosevelt said that beautiful young people are accidents of nature, but beautiful old people are works of art. She's implying that beauty in old age doesn't just happen. Our faces become what we've chosen to make them throughout our lives.

    • What expression do you want your face to have when you're 80 years old?

    • What changes, if any, do you need to make now in order to achieve your goal?

2. Describe the legacy you hope to leave. Again, what changes might be necessary in order to achieve that goal?

3. What fears do you face regarding growing old?

> The godly will flourish like palm trees
>   and grow strong like the cedars of Lebanon.
> For they are transplanted into the LORD's own house.
>   They flourish in the courts of our God.
> Even in old age they will still produce fruit;
>   they will remain vital and green.
> They will declare, "The LORD is just!
>   He is my rock!
>   There is nothing but goodness in him!"
> (Psalm 92:12).

4. According to this verse, how does God view old age? Describe the attitude of those who are fruitful in their old age.

5. Name an elderly woman who personifies Psalm 92:12-15. Describe her character qualities.

✦ PROMISES TO PONDER ✦

Yes, you have been with me from birth;
    from my mother's womb you have cared for me.
No wonder I am always praising you!
My life is an example to many,
    because you have been my strength and protection.
That is why I can never stop praising you;
    I declare your glory all day long...
Now that I am old and gray,
    do not abandon me, O God.
Let me proclaim your power to this new generation,
    your mighty miracles to all who come after me
(Psalm 71:6-8,18).

God is our refuge and strength,
    always ready to help in times of trouble.
So we will not fear, even if earthquakes come
    and the mountains crumble into the sea...
You will keep on guiding me with your counsel,
    leading me to a glorious destiny.
Whom have I in heaven but you?
    I desire you more than anything on earth.
My health may fail, and my spirit may grow weak,
    but God remains the strength of my heart;
    he is mine forever (Psalm 46:1-2; 73:24-26).

Though our bodies are dying, our spirits are being renewed every day...For we know that when this earthly

tent we live in is taken down—when we die and leave
these bodies—we will have a home in heaven, an eternal
body made for us by God himself and not by human
hands (2 Corinthians 4:16; 5:1).

✦ PRAYING THE PROMISES ✦

*Heavenly Father, You have cared for me from the time I
was in my mother's womb. Thank You for being my strength
and protection and for making my life an example to those
who are watching. Now, in my old age, please give me continued opportunities to declare Your glory and power. Use
my life as a testimony of Your mighty miracles to the next
generation. Amen.*

*Dear God, I praise You for being my refuge and strength.
I will not fear, regardless of my frightening circumstances,
because You are always ready to help me in times of trouble.
Guide me with Your counsel; lead me to a glorious destiny—
eternity with You! You are the strength of my heart, and
You are mine forever. Amen.*

*Father, my body is aging, but because of what You've done
for me through Jesus Christ, my spirit is being renewed
every day. When fear of aging and death grips me, help
me remember that my body is only a tent. My true home is
in heaven, and when I get there, You'll give me an eternal
body that You've made by Your own hands. Thank You for
giving me hope for eternity. Amen.*

From Fear *to* Faith

> What can counter and overcome
> our fears? Another fear! The fear of God,
> the glorious realization that He is bigger
> than all of our phobias and fears.
>
> JILL BRISCOE

From the sight of a daddy longlegs tiptoeing across the living room carpet or a foot-long garter snake slithering through the garden, to the threats of nuclear warfare, cancer, and child abduction by Internet predators, the list of fears women face seems endless. Sometimes our fear is based on that which is tangible—a weapon-wielding person or a natural disaster such as a flood or fire that threatens bodily harm and the loss of material possessions. Sometimes our behavior and attitudes are influenced by internal, invisible fears, such as the fear of rejection or of inadequacy. Regardless of the source, fear can paralyze us if we let it. But that need not be the case. There's a better way to navigate life!

In the midst of our fears, we can experience freedom by filling our minds with the truth about who God is and calling out to Him for help. When we do that, fear is no longer our enemy and becomes an opportunity for us to experience God in new ways. Acknowledging our dependence on Him and trusting Him to fulfill His promises gives us the privilege of seeing Him work on our behalf in ways we never could have imagined.

The foundational truth about God's character is that He is love. We're not talking about the fickle emotion so common among humans, but a divine unconditional love that supersedes anything on earth—a love so deep that it drove Him to make the ultimate sacrifice to restore the broken relationship between Himself and sinful mankind. "God showed how much he loved us by sending his only Son into the world so that we might have eternal life through him. This is real love. It is not that we loved God, but that he loved us and sent his Son as a sacrifice to take away our sins" (1 John 4:9-10).

Believing that God is love and that His love extends to us despite our sinfulness is the first step toward rising above our fears. Why? Because knowing the intensity of His love for us allows us to release our worries and rest in His care. If someone loves us so much that He's willing to die on our behalf, we know we can trust Him implicitly regardless of what happens. "Such love has no fear because perfect love expels all fear" (1 John 4:18).

If you've read the allegory *Hinds' Feet on High Places,* you'll remember the story's main character, Much-Afraid. A servant of the Chief Shepherd, she lived with her relatives—the Fearings—in the Valley of Humiliation. One day the Shepherd invited her to leave the valley and travel to the High Places, where no Fears can dwell. Before Much-Afraid could begin her trek, however, the Good Shepherd said she must allow Him to plant the seed of true Love in her heart.

"If I let you plant the seed of Love in my heart will you give me the promise that I shall be loved in return?" asked Much-Afraid. The Good Shepherd promised that this would be so.

> A thrill of joy went through her from head to foot. It seemed too wonderful to be believed, but the Shepherd himself was making the promise, and of one thing she

was quite sure. He could not lie. "Please plant Love in my heart now," she said faintly. Poor little soul, she was still Much-Afraid even when promised the greatest thing in the world.

The Shepherd put his hand in his bosom, drew something forth, and laid it in the palm of his hand. Then he held his hand out toward Much-Afraid. "Here is the seed of Love," he said.[1]

How about you? Are you like Much-Afraid, living with the Fearings in the Valley of Humiliation? If so, have you asked the Good Shepherd to plant the seed of His love in your heart so you can rise to the High Places where no Fears dwell?

Throughout this book, you've read stories about other women, the specific fears they've faced, and their experience of God's love in the midst of them. Perhaps you have an established relationship with God. But amid life's scary stuff, you've lost sight of His power at work in you and on your behalf. Unpleasant circumstances have loomed like giants and left you sick with worry or feeling as though God has forgotten about you.

Maybe you don't yet have a personal relationship with God. When scary stuff has come your way, you've tried to deny it or forget it by using alcohol or drugs. You've sought comfort in food or relied on your best friend to carry you through. Maybe you've turned to the horoscope for help or even considered taking your own life. Maybe you've never considered calling on God for help because you haven't known what to say or you've felt too undeserving.

Regardless of your situation or the fears you're struggling with, God wants to plant His love in your heart. Will you let Him do what He's come to do? Or will you turn Him away, afraid to let go and trust an unseen God to look after you? I encourage you to face *that* fear today and take the plunge. Trust God to catch you. Trust Him with your life, and you'll find Him faithful.

One of my favorite perks in this ministry is meeting women

from all walks of life. Each one has a story to tell. Some move me to tears; others make me laugh. My favorites are those that show God's power to transform lives when women understand and respond to His love. Rather than keep these stories to myself, I asked several gals for permission to share them with you. Each replied with a resounding "Yes!" Our desire is for every reader to see and understand that God can be trusted and that He will meet us in the midst of our fears.

Sue

On October 2, 1999, Sue was working in a tiny seaside cubicle, selling tickets to passengers traveling by ferry from Vancouver Island to a neighboring island. She'd spoken to her 13-year-old son, Jade, by phone a few minutes prior and looked forward to seeing him and her 15-year-old daughter, Heidi, when she returned home later that evening. A single mom, she loved her kids deeply. And she was determined to make their home life as stable as possible, unlike the environment she'd known as a child.

Sue had grown up in a family that stressed religious deeds. She'd attended church services and confession sessions with her mom and siblings every week. At home, they burned candles and knelt to recite prayers. But these rituals never made sense to Sue, especially considering the havoc that reigned in their household.

Her dad, a pharmacist, was an alcoholic. He'd come home from work, plop onto the couch with a case of beer between his feet, and drink himself into oblivion every evening. In the morning, he'd get up and return to work. He rarely spoke to his family.

Her mother was prone to depression and tried to commit suicide several times. She instilled many of her fears into Sue, including the fear that "if you do something bad, God is going to get you." She also insisted that Sue, her youngest child, be her constant companion. That changed when Sue was 15 years old and her mom transferred her affections to her first grandbaby.

Sue responded to her newfound freedom by pursuing a lifestyle saturated with drugs, alcohol, and promiscuity. For the next 15 years, she floated from one relationship to another, concerned only for her personal happiness at the moment. During that time she had two abortions and two miscarriages.

Finally Sue met a man with whom she fell in love. When she bore his daughter out of wedlock, she figured she'd best have the baby baptized as a religious safeguard. *After all,* she reasoned, *I don't want God to punish me or my baby for doing something bad.* When the baptism was over, she and her friends sat around drinking and smoking pot as usual. And so Sue's life continued for several years until one night when she awoke to find two strangers in her bathroom, injecting drugs. Her boyfriend, while visiting a bar that night, had given them permission to be there.

The experience frightened Sue. *I don't want to live this kind of life anymore,* she thought. *I need to change.* She began attending Alcoholics Anonymous, where she heard about a loving, caring God—unlike the God who she believed would "bite off your head or throw you in the depths of hell, or whatever, if you weren't good." She also quit smoking pot and cigarettes. But she knew something was lacking in her life.

Sue's kids began attending a church youth group when they reached their teenage years. Through that ministry, Jade, then 13, learned about Jesus Christ and chose to follow Him. He told Sue about his decision and tried to coax her to do the same, but she refused, thinking he was involved in a weird cult.

Then came October 2 and the heart-stopping phone call: "Jade's been hit by a car. The ambulance is on the way." The caller—a friend of Sue's—hung up, leaving her dumbfounded and numb. Not knowing who to call for help, she stepped outside the booth, looked at the sky, and said, "If You save my son, and he's not head-injured, I'll do anything for You."

Jade spent a week in the hospital and underwent two surgeries. When he was released, Sue told a Christian friend, "I told God that I would do anything for Him. Now what do I do?"

Her girlfriend said, "Are you willing to accept Him as your Savior?"

"Yes!" said Sue. Eight days after her son's near-fatal accident, she bowed her head and committed her life to Jesus Christ.

That was in 1999. Sue's former life is long gone. Now she attends church weekly because she wants to, not because she's afraid of displeasing an angry God who will "get her" if she doesn't. She loves reading His Word and encouraging others to do the same, and she rejoices that both of her kids are following Jesus.

Sue loves looking for opportunities to share God's love with others. She serves on the board of directors for the local pregnancy center and volunteers at her community's soup kitchen, praying with the men and women who come seeking spiritual help. She considers her car a vehicle for ministry, so she gives rides to stranded motorists and folks who need a lift. Occasionally she visits and prays with residents at her town's roughest inn, where round-the-clock security guards wear bulletproof vests. And whenever possible, she spends Friday evenings sharing hot meals and prayers with exotic dancers at a local bar. The first time she entered the building for ministry, she cried for 20 minutes because she realized afresh what God had delivered her from.

"He *is* my Savior," says Sue today. "I lived in the blackest world you could possibly imagine, and He loved me enough to rescue me."[2]

Pamela

Pamela was 21 years old when she met her prince. His name was Christian, and he was everything she'd wished for in a husband. When they married, she felt confident that he would always love her, always protect her, and always be there for her.

Having that security was important to Pamela. While growing up, she'd enjoyed a loving relationship with her father until her older siblings became teenagers and his attention shifted to them. In a small way, she felt as though he'd abandoned her, and she didn't want to experience the same disappointment again.

Christian worked in a law firm, and Pamela stayed home to raise their four children. Fourteen years passed, and they appeared to be set to live happily ever after. But the fairy tale turned to a nightmare when Christian began displaying worrisome physical symptoms.

"Parkinson's disease," said the doctors.

Pamela's worst fears came true. She visualized her husband with an "out of order" sign hanging around his neck. He was broken, unable to protect her and be her strength, unable to be there for her. An invisible wall went up between them as Pamela struggled to see and embrace the man behind the debilitating disease.

Christian's health deteriorated rapidly, so Pamela stepped into the role of financial provider. She established a health and wellness teaching and training company from her home, enabling her to be available for her husband and kids. She poured her energy into the business for five years, and it prospered. But as it did, it became a mistress to her. In her own words, she became a selfish, ambitious machine, trying to fill her emotional void with fame and success, but she felt increasingly empty.

At one point, Pamela began training a woman who wanted to join the business. When the woman observed the family's desperate situation, she invited Pamela to attend church with her.

Church? thought Pamela. *I haven't been to church since our wedding, and that was 19 years ago!* Nevertheless, she agreed, thinking she was doing her employee a favor by accepting her invitation.

Pamela had attended services every Sunday as a child because her parents considered it important, but she'd found the experience unfulfilling. After she and Christian married, they agreed to forego church attendance. Pamela believed that God was out there somewhere, but she'd never been taught about having a relationship with Him. Now, as she listened to the preacher, her heart stirred, and she knew God was speaking directly to her.

"Jesus is the rock," said the preacher. "He's the same yesterday, today, and forever. No matter what happens in the world, Jesus is the same. He does not change."

That's what I want, thought Pamela. *My dad shifted, my husband shifted. I need Someone who will always be the same.*

Pamela returned home recalling the things she'd heard in church as a little girl. *God is holy and I'm not, so I'd best make myself pure before I try having a relationship with Him,* she thought. She spent the next month trying to think good thoughts and to put others' needs before her own. She tried to be unselfish and to suppress any ambition for personal gain. It didn't work. She failed miserably from hour to hour. That's when she remembered other words the preacher had said: "Come to Jesus just as you are. He will make you clean. His Spirit will come into you and help you be like Him on a daily basis."

At that instant, Pamela knew she must give her life to Jesus. A quick phone call to her business associate's church resulted in an invitation for her to drop by the pastor's home. He explained what it meant to follow Jesus and asked if she was serious about her desire to do so.

"Yes, yes, YES!" said Pamela. "Let's pray now, please!" The pastor prayed, and Pamela repeated his words. She gave God her dreams and hopes, and she invited Him to take control of her future. She sensed Him washing her with His love on the inside and filling her with His Spirit.

Pamela rushed home to tell her husband about her decision to follow Christ. When she entered his bedroom, she saw beyond the disease to the man she loved. The barrier was gone. Her selfishness, her self-pity, and her own longings and needs evaporated. All that remained was a desire to love and serve Christian, to help him and nurture him, and be by his side.

Thirteen years later, Pamela embraces the same perspective. She spends almost all of her time at home, caring for Christian. She admits that doing so would be impossible without God's strength. "I used to think of his illness as being an overwhelming circumstance I was called to bear. I tried to use success to dull the pain, but it only widened the gap between my husband and me," she says. "Now

I consider caring for my husband as my call. With the call comes God's grace, and His strength, and His equipping and enabling. God promises to supply all our needs according to His glorious riches in Christ Jesus, and I believe His promises are true."

Pamela recently enjoyed the opportunity to attend a musical concert. As she listened to the performance and marveled at the musician's talent, a thought crossed her mind: *What song are you playing with your life?*

None, thought Pamela. *I've never devoted myself to learning to play an instrument.*

Oh, but you are *playing a song,* the Lord seemed to say. *For five years you tried to deal with your husband's illness in your own strength, and it didn't work. Then you surrendered to Jesus. He placed a sheet of music called Parkinson's disease on the piano of your life. The notes are impossible to play. But Jesus is sitting on the bench. When you don't know how to play the notes, just put your hands on His. He will move you through the difficult melodies that are in this particular piece He's asked you to play. When you do so, you play beautiful music.*

Pamela smiled. She continues to smile, and for good reason. Christian committed his life to Jesus in 2002. His body is still "out of order," but his inner man is strong. They often lie on his bed for short periods and listen to Scripture on audio tape, or Pamela recites a passage to her husband. Then they talk about what the Lord impressed on their hearts through it.

Pamela's fairy tale has a different ending from the one she'd imagined. Her circumstances grow more difficult as her husband's illness progresses, but she knows Jesus, the One who will never change or leave her. And that relationship gives her strength, joy, and hope.[3]

Sarah

Life in Sarah's home seemed relatively normal, other than the presence of witchcraft books her dad kept on a shelf. But Sarah wasn't bothered by them or by knowing that her dad thought he possessed special powers and believed in reincarnation. She'd been taught that people could believe whatever they wanted. As for her, she chose to believe that a God existed out there somewhere but that He wasn't interested in her.

Things started going haywire when Sarah turned 14. Until then she'd enjoyed a close relationship with her father. But then a woman moved into an upstairs apartment in her family's home, bringing cocaine with her. Before long, Sarah's dad became a user. At first, Sarah didn't want to admit what she was seeing. But one night everything came to an explosive head.

Sarah's dad, high on drugs, was convinced that spies lived in the attic and in the trees surrounding the house. He saw objects in the house trying to attack the family. Sarah's mom took the younger daughter and fled for safety, leaving Sarah behind. Her dad then loaded two shotguns and shooed Sarah from the house to check the trees for spies. She obeyed, but when she returned to the house, she found the door locked.

Banging on the door resulted in a window shattering, which led to Sarah staring down the barrel of a loaded shotgun. *I no longer have a dad,* she thought at that moment. *My dad is gone.* Thankfully, the police arrived and took her father to a detox center for the weekend. But when he returned, her parents acted as if nothing had happened.

The incident shook Sarah. She no longer trusted her dad, and she felt as though her mom didn't care about her well-being, so she began her quest to find whatever could make life work. She began her search with the witchcraft books on the shelf. Her parents seemed pleased with her initiative, so they encouraged her by buying more books, incense, tarot cards, and anything else she wanted for her collection.

The dabbling became a passion, and soon Sarah was involved in séances, spells, and a personal spirit guide whom she named Jesus. But nothing worked. Life felt more confused than ever. Rather than finding peace and comfort, she fell into depression. She felt convinced that suicide was her only recourse and that if she died, she could enjoy a fresh beginning. She attempted suicide twice but failed.

That's when she decided to leave home and head for college. As only God could have ordained it, her two roommates were Christian girls. Sarah observed their attitudes and behavior. She watched as they read their Bibles and prayed. She admitted that they possessed the peace she so desperately craved.

When the roommates started a Bible study, Sarah attended. When they invited her to go to an InterVarsity meeting, she went. She listened, captivated, as the speaker challenged the audience to lay their lives on the altar as sacrifices to God. As a teenage witch, she was well acquainted with the concept of altars and sacrifices, but she'd never heard it presented like this.

When the meeting ended, Sarah went for a walk on campus. She dropped to her knees on the grass, looked up at the sky and thought, *There's so much I don't understand. If there really is a God, what do I do about it? What's my choice?* Then she said, *God, if You're real and You actually want me, I'm Yours.*

As Sarah describes it, God reached down with His hand and pulled her from a pit. Foul language, heavy drinking, and other habits slowly disappeared as she began reading her Bible. She and several Christian friends burned her witchcraft paraphernalia. She began understanding that God's love is a gift, not a favor to be earned. And she began to comprehend His promise to never abandon her. That truth became especially meaningful when her parents expressed anger and feelings of betrayal at her decision to follow Jesus Christ.

Today Sarah is a thirtysomething wife and mother of three young daughters. She's also a writer, and that's the fulfillment of a lifelong dream. Throughout her growing-up years, she thought writing a book someday would be wonderful. That hope was shattered in high school when someone told her she lacked the necessary talent. She buried her desire and turned her focus toward other interests.

Several years passed. After she married, she and her husband were working with their church's youth when a story idea came to mind. It was about a teenage girl who attended a youth group and pretended she was a Christian. Sarah began typing, and she wrote on and off for several months until she completed the book. To her amazement, a publisher asked for that manuscript and several more. So far, she's written five books in that series and has developed an online ministry with her teen audience.

Sarah's journey began with a belief that yes, God existed, but He wasn't interested in her. Today she admits that was far from the truth. He loved her enough to guide her to the truth, and the truth set her free.[4]

Barbara

Barbara's father entered her bedroom after midnight. "C'mon. Wake up. We're leaving," he said. Five-year-old Barbara rubbed her eyes and crawled from her bed. Her mother shooed her and her two younger brothers into the backseat of their family car, and they left town. The scene was a familiar one, having repeated itself about nine times before. Townsfolk frowned on unpaid bills, and unpaid bills were her dad's specialty. Moving from state to state provided escape from the law.

But one day Barbara's dad left home alone—for good. Three years later, her mother dropped her and her brothers at a so-called foster home and drove away. The kids suffered emotional and sexual abuse until her mother returned two years later. But living with an alcoholic mother who had a weakness for abusive men made childhood anything but pleasant.

Barbara left home after high school, intent on gaining control of her circumstances and swearing she'd never be like her mother. She married, trained to become a Montessori teacher, and gave birth to a daughter. On the outside she appeared bold and brazen, but that tough exterior was like survival gear and masked the hidden fear that her life was worthless.

She rose to leadership in the feminist movement, protested war, rallied for abortion rights, and dabbled in Eastern religions. Along the way, she gave birth to another daughter, but she also began using and selling drugs and participating in the free sex movement. Before long she'd convinced herself that her husband was holding her back from realizing her creative genius. She bid him and their eldest child goodbye, abandoning her daughter just as her own mother had deserted her years prior.

Barbara's downward spiral steepened. One day she woke from an alcohol-induced blackout and, falling to her knees beside her bed, cried: *God! Help me! I'm an alcoholic, and I'm going to die if I keep drinking.* Hours later she attended her first Alcoholics Anonymous meeting and heard about the concept of a personal God. That triggered her curiosity, and she launched a quest to seek Him, but she delved into Eastern religions rather than Christianity—a religion she scorned, based on others' opinions rather than her own study.

Barbara's spiritual journey intersected with Tripp, a man seven years her junior and a soul mate seeking God through yoga and meditation. Three months later, she was pregnant—a medical miracle after a serious infection had rendered her sterile. Barbara and Tripp had both been through abortion experiences, and they could have followed the same route again without a second thought. Instead, Tripp said, "We'll get married."

Years passed. Three sons were born, and Tripp and Barbara established a successful landscaping business. Things on the home front looked good to outsiders, but Barbara and Tripp knew otherwise.

Their spiritual journey had led them to believe that they were both God. They strove to achieve their divine potential and pursued their right to be happy. They practiced a variety of New Age beliefs, combined with bits and pieces of other philosophies. They expected their quest to bring harmony. Instead, it brought strife. With their marriage in turmoil, Barbara decided she'd made a mistake and she could create a better reality without Tripp.

God intervened. One morning while driving in her car, Barbara caught a *Focus on the Family* radio broadcast. She heard Dennis and Barbara Rainey, founders of FamilyLife ministry, discuss a weekend conference designed for married couples. Their enthusiasm and message of hope sparked Barbara's interest, and she decided to register.

Attending the conference healed their relationship, but it did something even better—it healed their souls. As Barbara discovered God's plan for marriage, she also heard about His plan for a personal relationship with her. She learned that she was not a divine being, but a sinner in need of a Savior. And she discovered that Jesus Christ had come to earth to be that Savior, dying on a cross and rising from the dead three days later to overcome sin and death once and for all. Tears streamed down her cheeks as she bowed her head and prayed silently, confessing that she was a sinner and inviting Jesus to take control of her life. Tripp did the same.

The couple returned home, eager to read the Bible. They burned their meditation altar and disposed of their New Age books, tapes, pictures, and idols. Peace replaced conflict in their home. Their children noticed the difference, and they too trusted Jesus for their salvation.

That was in 1987. Today, Barbara admits that fear dominated her former lifestyle, but she hadn't recognized it then. "When my parents abandoned me, I got the message that my life didn't matter. Drugs, alcohol, and sex anesthetized my emotional pain." She marvels at God's fingerprints of protection and mercy over her life even when she didn't recognize His presence.

"I don't look back and ask, 'Where was God when I needed Him?'" says Barbara. "I don't blame Him for allowing abuse—that's just the world we live in. When people don't know the Lord, they don't know any better. People hurt me, and I hurt others. In the midst of the garbage, God loved me and was drawing me to Himself."

Like the other women's stories, Barbara's reassures us of the hope and healing made possible through a relationship with Christ. It also shows how God can use our failures to accomplish good. In

Barbara's case, He's given her amazing opportunities to encourage mothers in their role and in their personal lives. She has written nine books meant for that purpose, and she writes a wisdom-dispensing blog that draws more than 2000 readers daily.[5]

Stories such as these give me a better appreciation of God's love for us. And Scripture makes the picture even more vivid!

> Say to those who are afraid, "Be strong, and do not fear, for your God is coming to destroy your enemies. He is coming to save you." And when he comes, he will open the eyes of the blind and unstop the ears of the deaf. The lame will leap like a deer, and those who cannot speak will shout and sing! Springs will gush forth in the wilderness, and streams will water the desert. The parched ground will become a pool, and springs of water will satisfy the thirsty land. Marsh grass and reeds and rushes will flourish where desert jackals once lived…Those who have been ransomed by the LORD will return to Jerusalem, singing songs of everlasting joy. Sorrow and mourning will disappear, and they will be overcome with joy and gladness (Isaiah 35:4-7,10).

Do not be afraid—God is coming to destroy your enemies. What are they? The fear of the unknown? The fear of financial insecurity? The fear for your child's well-being? Whatever fear-enemy you face, God wants to save you from it. He wants to take it from you and fill your life with freedom and joy and gladness instead. Let Him do what He's come to do.

Peace

"The oldest and strongest emotion of mankind is fear," said H.P. Lovecraft. I tend to agree with him. Every woman alive struggles with fear of one sort or another. For some, placing their lives into the hands of an unseen God is a terrifying thought. If you're one of these gals, let me reassure you that you'll never regret facing your fear and saying, *Here I am, God! I'm Yours!* Establishing a relationship with Him is the only way you'll experience Him as your source of strength and courage when other fears confront you. It's also the only way you'll find peace.

One of God's names is Jehovah Shalom—God of peace. He sent Jesus to die on the cross to purchase peace for us with Him. When our hearts are right with this holy God and sin's power over us is broken, we know the meaning of true peace. No longer do we need to seek its counterfeit in success, human relationships, outer beauty, or others' approval. Because we've been forgiven, no longer do we need to struggle with guilt or self-blame. Our hearts are at rest.

> The Lord, your Redeemer, the Holy One of Israel, says: I am the Lord your God, who teaches you what is good and leads you along the paths you should follow. Oh, that you had listened to my commands! Then you would have had peace flowing like a gentle river and righteousness rolling like waves (Isaiah 48:17-18).

We can also experience peace that passes logic when scary stuff happens, knowing that God loves us and holds us in His hands. Barb W. is a woman whose life demonstrates this God-given peace.

Terrified by needles as a young girl, she imagined that being diagnosed with diabetes would be equal to a death sentence. At age 17, her fears came true. The doctors told her she had diabetes, and she spent most of her senior year in the hospital. To complicate matters, fibromyalgia and chronic fatigue syndrome struck several years later. But that wasn't all. After 25 years of marriage, her husband told her that he didn't love her anymore and walked away.

Barb could have allowed fear to paralyze her. Instead, she chose to admit her fear of diabetes and of abandonment and believe that God would be her strength and provider. She'd grown up believing that He loved her, and she knew He wouldn't fail her now. And He hasn't.

"My scary situations have shown me that all I really need is God," says Barb today. "I'm happy where I am, and the joy of the Lord is so strong. More than anything, I have the peace that only God can give. He's helped me realize that my fears aren't worth a second glance."[6]

Dear reader, does your heart, like Barb's, have peace based on a relationship with Jesus? If not, I want to encourage you to consider God's words. Listen to His commands so that your peace will flow like a gentle river and your righteousness will roll like waves. What a beautiful picture of what He wants to accomplish in our lives!

Establishing a relationship with Jesus is not difficult. First, we need to admit that we're sinners. "For all have sinned; all fall short of God's glorious standard," Romans 3:23 says. In other words, we're all guilty of sins such as envy, gossip, cheating, lying, jealousy, thinking evil thoughts, and more.

Sin erects a barrier between us and the holy God. It also warrants the penalty of death. But in His mercy, God has stepped in and provided an alternative plan, a gift to anyone willing to accept it: "For the wages of sin is death, but the free gift of God is eternal life through Christ Jesus our Lord" (Romans 6:23).

God accomplished this by sending His Son, Jesus, to earth. While here, He lived a sinless life, yet He paid the penalty for our sins by dying on a cross. Three days later He rose from the grave to overcome death once and for all and to purchase both peace and a place in heaven for those who believe: "For God so loved the world that he gave his only Son, so that everyone who believes in him will not perish but have eternal life. God did not send his Son into the world to condemn it, but to save it" (John 3:16).

In order for us to secure that place, we simply have to believe in Jesus. That means more than believing He was a historical figure, like George Washington or Abraham Lincoln. They existed too, but they can't save us. Believing in Him means more than crying out to Him to get us out of a pinch or a crisis situation and then going on our merry way when the problem has passed. Believing in Jesus means placing our saving faith in Him alone rather than in good deeds or in a religious upbringing for eternal life.

If you would like to receive God's free gift of eternal life today, just tell Him so, or use this prayer as a guide:

> Dear God, I admit that I'm a sinner. I confess that I've broken Your law and deserve to be punished. But I believe that Jesus Christ paid my penalty when He died on the cross. And I believe that He rose from the dead three days later to purchase a place in heaven for me. Forgive my sins and save me. I accept Your free gift of salvation. Thank You! Amen.

If you have given your life to Jesus, you are a new creature: "Those who become Christians become new persons. They are not the same anymore, for the old life is gone. A new life has begun! All this newness of life is from God, who brought us back to himself through what Christ did" (2 Corinthians 5:17-18). You'll go through changes in thinking and behavior, just as the women in this chapter did. Some may be instant; others may take more time. God is interested in shaping your character to become like Jesus, and that doesn't happen overnight.

I want to encourage you to tell someone about your decision—your spouse, a Christian girlfriend, or the pastor of a Bible-teaching church. Read a Bible (I've quoted from the New Living Translation for this book), get involved with other believers for encouragement as you grow, talk to God throughout your day. He loves you so much, and He wants you to know Him intimately. He has good things in store for you, my dear!

If you're already a believer, I trust that you'll press on to know God. When fears roll in, refuse to let them paralyze you. Instead, call out to God and expect Him to answer. May your love for Him be deepened. May your trust in Him be strengthened. And may your understanding of who He is be expanded as you move from fear into freedom.

Do not fear anything except the LORD Almighty.
He alone is the Holy One. If you fear him, you need
fear nothing else (Isaiah 8:13).

See, God has come to save me.
    I will trust in him and not be afraid.
The LORD GOD is my strength and my song;
    he has become my salvation.

With joy you will drink deeply from the fountain of
    salvation! In that wonderful day you will sing:
"Thank the LORD!
    Praise his name!
Tell the world what he has done,
    Oh, how mighty he is!
Sing to the LORD,
    for he has done wonderful things.
    Make known his praise around the world
(Isaiah 12:2-5).

NOTES

Chapter 1—The Faces of Fear

1. *The American Heritage Dictionary of the English Language,* 4th ed., s.v. "phobia."
2. www.nimh.nih.gov/healthinformation/anxietymenu.cfm
3. Bruce Larson, *Living Beyond Our Fears* (San Fransisco: Harper & Row Publishers, 1990), 8.

Chapter 2—Our Kids' Well-Being

1. www.cdc.gov/ncipc/factsheets/poisoning.htm
2. www.cdc.gov/ncipc/factsheets/playgr.htm
3. Carol Kent, *Tame Your Fears* (Colorado Springs: Navpress, 2003), 31.
4. Phone interview.
5. Thomas O. Chisholm, "Great Is Thy Faithfulness," copyright 1923, 1951 by Hope Publishing Company, Carol Stream, IL. All rights reserved. Used by permission.

Chapter 3—Don't Touch My Stuff!

1. Phone interview.
2. Wesley K. Willmer, *God and Your Stuff* (Colorado Springs: Navpress, 2002), 9.
3. David Wilkerson, *Knowing God by Name* (Grand Rapids: Chosen Books, 2003), 26.
4. Ibid., 28.
5. E-mail interview.
6. Rick Joyner, *Overcoming Fear* (Wilkesboro, NC: MorningStar Publications, 2002), 35.
7. Ibid., 46.

8. Phone interview.

9. Phone interview.

10. "Top Ten Grocery Savings Tips," copyright 2003 by Ellie Kay. Used by permission.

11. Karen O'Connor, *Addicted to Shopping* (Eugene, OR: Harvest House Publishers, 2005), 20.

Chapter 4—Lessons Learned in the Storm

1. Grace Fox, "Taking a Stand," *Power for Living,* May 29, 2005.

2. Bruce Larson, *Living Beyond Our Fears* (San Fransisco: Harper & Row Publishers, 1990), 9.

3. Phone interview.

4. John Ortberg, *If You Want to Walk on Water, You've Got to Get Out of the Boat* (Grand Rapids: Zondervan, 2001), 162.

5. Ibid., 161.

6. Jerry Bridges, "Can I Really Trust God?" *Discipleship Journal,* Issue 130, 2002, 54.

7. Kenneth W. Osbeck, *101 Hymn Stories* (Grand Rapids: Kregel Publications, 1982), 57-58.

8. Max Lucado, *In the Eye of the Storm* (Dallas: Word Publishing, 1991), 164-165.

Chapter 5—What Will Tomorrow Bring?

1. Grace Fox, "Shining in the Shadows," *Power for Living,* July 17, 2005. Visit Jennifer's ministry website at www.jenniferrothschild.com.

2. John Ortberg, *If You Want to Walk on Water, You've Got to Get Out of the Boat* (Grand Rapids: Zondervan, 2001), 192.

3. Max Lucado, "Tomorrow's Dream, Today's Courage," available online at www.maxlucado.com/pdf/tomorrow.pdf.

4. Phone interview.

5. Katie Brazelton, *Pathway to Purpose for Women* (Grand Rapids: Zondervan, 2005), 212.

6. John Ortberg, *If You Want to Walk on Water,* 157.

7. Cited in "In God We Trust," *Today's Christian Woman,* January/February 2002, 42.

8. Sherri Langton, "Facing the Future Without Fear," *Discipleship Journal,* July/August 1999, 29.

9. Katie Brazelton, *Pathway to Purpose for Women,* 208.

10. Nancy Leigh DeMoss, *Surrender: The Heart God Controls* (Chicago: Moody Publishers, 2003), 124.

Chapter 6—Who, Me?

1. Henry T. Blackaby and Claude V. King, *Experiencing God Workbook* (Nashville: LifeWay Press, 1990), 108.

2. Ibid., 153.

3. Donna J. Shepherd, "Turning Fear into Faith," *Just Between Us,* summer 2003, 20.

4. Gary Thomas, "Finding Fortitude," *Discipleship Journal,* Issue 130, 2002, 36.

5. Donna Partow, *Walking in Total God-Confidence* (Minneapolis: Bethany House Publishers, 1999), 58.

6. John Ortberg *If You Want to Walk on Water, You've Got to Get Out of the Boat* (Grand Rapids: Zondervan, 2001), 43.

7. Donna Partow, *Walking in Total God-Confidence,* 49.

8. Pam Farrel, *Woman of Influence* (Downers Grove: InterVarsity Press, 2006), 132.

9. A.W. Tozer, *The Pursuit of God* (Harrisburg, PA: Christian Publications, Inc., 1948), 116.

10. Personal interview.

11. Rebecca Manley Pippert, *A Heart Like His* (Wheaton: Crossway Books, 1996), 35.

12. James Alexander Langteaux, *God.Net* (Sisters, OR: Multnomah Publishers, 2001), 230.

13. Phone interview.

14. John Ortberg, "Stepping Out," *Servant Magazine,* Fall 2002, 7.

15. Donna Partow, *Walking in Total God-Confidence,* 55.

Chapter 7—Will You Love the Real Me?

1. Data collected by pro-abortion organizations and quoted by the Center for Bio-Ethical Reform; www.cbrinfo.org/Resources/fastfacts.html.

2. A.W. Tozer, *The Pursuit of God* (Harrisburg, PA: Christian Publications, Inc., 1948), 114.

3. Marilyn Meberg, *The Zippered Heart* (Nashville: W Publishing Group, 2001), 189-190.

4. Phone interview. Names have been changed to protect privacy.

5. Brennan Manning, "Living as God's Beloved," *Discipleship Journal,* July/August 1997, 74.

6. Henri Nouwen, *Life of the Beloved* (New York: Crossroad Publishing, 1992), 27.

7. Marilyn Meberg, *The Zippered Heart*, 192.

8. Brennan Manning, "Living as God's Beloved," 75.

9. Phone interview.

10. Beth Moore, "Overcoming the Insecurity of Feeling Unloved," *HomeLife*, October 2000, 30.

11. Ibid., 31.

Chapter 8—Saying Goodbye to the Ghosts in My Past

1. Phone interview. Visit Jana's website at www.janalapel.com.

2. Liz Curtis Higgs, *Bad Girls of the Bible* (Colorado Springs: WaterBrook Press, 1999), 79.

3. Sue Augustine, *When Your Past Is Hurting Your Present* (Eugene, OR: Harvest House Publishers, 2005), 108-109.

4. Phone interview.

5. Phone interview.

6. Gayle G. Roper, "I Can't Forgive Myself," *Discipleship Journal*, May/June 1997, 32. Adapted with author's permission.

7. Phone interview. Visit Mac's website at www.NightshiftMinistries.org.

8. Gordon MacDonald, "Questions I'd Ask Before Following Jesus," *Discipleship Journal,* July/August 1997, 33.

9. Phone interview.

Chapter 9—It's Not About Gray Hair and Wrinkles

1. Cited in M. Greengrass, "Attitudes about aging affect longevity, study says." Available online at www.apa.org/monitor/oct02/attitudes.

2. Cecil Murphey, *Aging Is an Attitude* (Chattanooga: AMG Publishers, 2005), 9.

3. Marni Jackson, "Suitable Reflections," *Reader's Digest,* January 2004, 32.

4. Phone interview.

5. Cited in Nicholas Read, "Pain Is an Epidemic," *The Vancouver Sun,* August 26, 2006.

6. Phone interview.

7. Phone interview.

8. Linda Kohn, Janet Corrigan, and Molla Donaldsen, eds., *To Err Is Human* (Washington, DC: National Academy Press Institute of Medicine, 1999), 22.

9. Phone interview.

Chapter 10—From Fear to Faith

1. Hannah Hurnard, *Hinds' Feet on High Places* (Wheaton: Tyndale House Publishers, Inc., 1975), 26.
2. Phone interview.
3. Phone interview.
4. Phone interview. Visit Sarah's website at www.sarahannesumpolec.com.
5. Phone interview. Visit Barbara's blog at www.mommylife.net.
6. Personal interview.

Other Great Harvest House Books
by Grace Fox

10-Minute Time Outs for Moms

Insightful devotions from author and mother Grace Fox empower you to maintain a vital connection with God. Inspiring stories, Scripture-based prayers, and practical guidance offer you strength for your spiritual journey and daily life.

10-Minute Time Outs for Busy Women

Grace Fox encourages you to make time for what matters most—your relationship with God. Her real-life stories and Scripture-based prayers will help you understand God's truth and apply it to everyday life.

10-Minute Time Outs for You and Your Kids

Grace provides engaging stories, activities, and prayers in a welcoming format you can use to lead your family to the riches of God's Word and sharing time together—in 10 minutes.

If you would like to share your story with Grace or invite her to speak to your church, women's group, conference, or retreat, visit her website at www.gracefox.com.

To learn more about Harvest House books
or to read sample chapters, log on to our website:

www.harvesthousepublishers.com

HARVEST HOUSE PUBLISHERS

EUGENE, OREGON